**The Japanese
Economic System**

The Japanese Economic System

An Institutional Overview

Kanji Haitani
State University of New York

Lexington Books
D. C. Heath and Company
Lexington, Massachusetts
Toronto

Library of Congress Cataloging in Publication Data

Haitani, Kanji.
  The Japanese economic system.

  Includes index.
  1. Japan—Economic conditions—1945–   2. Social
institutions—Japan. I. Title.
HC462.9.H17   330.9′52′04   76-11972
ISBN 0-669-00716-1

Published simultaneously in Canada

Printed in the United States of America

International Standard Book Number: 0-669-00716-1

Library of Congress Catalog Card Number: 76-11972

To Masako

Contents

List of Figures

List of Tables

Preface

My reason for writing this book is to provide basic and descriptive information on how the Japanese economic system is organized and how it works. I have tried to describe in simple language the institutional topography of the heartland of the Japanese economy in a way that stresses its historical, social, and cultural aspects. The emphasis of the book is not on the performance of the economy, but on institutions—primarily economic, but also political and social. The Japanese economic system is perceived not as a "GNP machine" but as a sum total of the ways in which the Japanese people manage their economic affairs.

It is hoped that this book will be found useful by the students of the Japanese society, economy, government, and business. Specifically, my aim has been to provide a readable textbook for college courses in Asian studies and comparative economic systems.

I would like to express my appreciation to my friends who read and commented on part of earlier chapters. Joe Camerata, Al Conely, Marwan El Nasser, Rick Lundquist, Patricia Netherly, and Jim Soukup have been particularly helpful. Naturally they are in no way responsible for any of the book's imperfections. I would also like to thank all the persons in Japan who took time to discuss with me the Japanese economy and its problems during my two-month stay there in the summer of 1974. Thanks are also due to my mother, Mrs. Toyoko Haitani, and my sister-in-law, Ms. Sachiko Yokota of the Seto Municipal Library, for having kept me supplied with Japanese source materials. My deepest gratitude is due to my wife Masako and my children, Linda Naoko and Robert Yuji. Without their encouragement, cooperation, and tolerance, this book would not have been written.

**The Japanese
Economic System**

1 Introduction

An economic system consists of the economic institutions of a society. An *institution* is a sum total of the ways in which social units (individuals, families, business firms, or government agencies) are expected to act or interact. By *economic* we mean that which pertains to man's material well-being. Thus, the Japanese economic system is simply the total set of the ways in which the Japanese people, individually and collectively, look after their material well-being.

An economic system cannot exist in a vacuum. It is surrounded by its particular political environment, and the whole politicoeconomic complex is immersed in the sociocultural environment. The ways in which a nation organizes its economic activities, therefore, are uniquely determined by its social and cultural factors. The study of an economic system accomplishes little if it fails to examine how these "exogenous" factors affect the economy.

There is a general agreement among sociologists and anthropologists that the most pronounced difference between Japan and the West is the former's strong familial collectivism orientation. Individuals are bound together in a web of human obligations and draw strength and security from a group to which they belong—be it a family, school, or business firm. Individuals, in the traditional Japanese view, are like waves in an ocean; a wave does not exist outside of the mass of water that is society. Smaller waves form a larger wave, and all the waves are organically related to each other; in fact, an individual wave is a transcendental manifestation of the whole itself.

In a modern, technologically complex society, collectivist approaches are often superior to the rugged individualism of earlier times. The whole is quite often more than a sum of the parts, and the Western emphasis on teamwork implicitly recognizes this fact. Japanese groupism, however, involves more than an emphasis on teamwork; it is based on deep emotional ties between the hierarchically related members of a group as well as on an equally strong emotional rejection of outsiders. Naturally, Japan's familial groupism exhibits strengths and weaknesses that are not found in more individualistically oriented Western societies.

Not all economic institutions are equally affected by the social and cultural factors. The financial institutions in Japan, for example, are more similar to their Western counterparts than, say, the employment relations. As a general rule, we may say that the more *human* the relations

1

are, the greater the potential difference between the Japanese and the Western ways.

This book describes Japan's major economic institutions and their political environment, and provides interpretations of these aspects in the light of the uniquely Japanese sociocultural background. In this introductory chapter, we start with the realities of the land, the people, and the economy; we then proceed to briefly examine the key features of the Japanese political system and the two-thousand-year history of Japan.

Economic and Human Geography

The island nation of Japan consists of four main islands (Honshu, Hokkaido, Kyushu, and Shikoku) lying in the North Pacific Ocean off the east coast of Asia. These islands extend in a southwest-northeast direction for a distance of about 1,200 miles. The total land area of Japan is approximately 146,000 square miles, which is slightly smaller than the state of California but considerably larger than Italy. The country's terrain is mostly mountainous. Only about 18 percent of the total area is arable, and 15 percent is cultivated. The only mineral resource that exists in abundance is sulfur. In 1970, about 85 percent of the country's natural gas requirement, 90 percent of copper and iron ore, over 99 percent of oil, and 100 percent of bauxite, nickel, and uranium had to be imported.

The population of Japan in October 1975 was 111.9 million. The annual rate of population increase in the 1970s has been about 1.3 percent. Tokyo, the nation's capital, had a population of 11.7 million. Population and industrial activities are concentrated in the Pacific coastal area on the Island of Honshu. Known as the Pacific Industrial Belt, this 300-mile corridor contains Japan's six largest cities and accounts for more than one-third of its population and three-quarters of its national output.

Since the mid-1960s, the Japanese economy has been the third largest in the world. Japan's gross national product (GNP) in 1975 was about $483 billion; this was about one-third of the United States' GNP, and larger than that of all Asia put together, including China and India.[a] Japan's GNP per capita—$4,330 in 1975—was roughly equal to that of the Soviet Union, and was larger than that of Britain or Italy.

In 1973, about 47 percent of Japan's total population was gainfully employed. The percentage distribution of the labor force and national product by industry is shown in Table 1–1. Primary industries employed 13.4 percent of the labor force and produced only 7.1 percent of national

---

[a]The yen values are converted into dollar values at an exchange rate of ¥300 = $1. This rate will be used throughout this book unless otherwise noted.

Table 1–1
Net Domestic Product and Labor Force, by Industry, 1973
(Percent)

Industry	Net Domestic Product	Labor Force
Primary industries[a]	7.1%	13.4%
Secondary industries	36.7	36.7
Mining	0.5	0.4
Manufacturing	27.7	27.4
Construction	8.5	8.9
Tertiary industries	56.3	49.8
Transport, communication, and utilities	7.3	7.1
Wholesale and retail trade	17.8 ⎫	
	⎬	23.6
Banking, insurance, and real estate	12.9 ⎭	
Services	14.1	15.7
Public administration	4.2	3.4

Source: Bank of Japan, Statistics Department, *Economic Statistics Annual, 1974*, pp. 257–258, 297–298.
[a] Agriculture, forestry, and fishing.

product; the discrepancy in these two ratios implies the low labor productivity in these industries. The proportion of labor force in the primary industries is perhaps the best indicator of a nation's level of industrial development. In Japan, this ratio was 41.0 percent in 1958. It had fallen to 24.6 percent by 1965, and further to 13.4 percent by 1973. This rapid decline in the primary-industry ratio was a concomitant of the rapid growth of the Japanese economy; it grew at an annual rate of 10 percent in real terms between the early 1950s and 1973. By way of comparison, we may note that the primary-industry ratios of the United States and the United Kingdom in 1973 were about 4 percent and 3 percent, respectively. Japan's 13.4 percent ratio for 1973, therefore, implies that the economy still has some distance to cover before it reaches the industrial maturity of the United States and the United Kingdom.

The Political System

Japan is a parliamentary democracy, patterned largely after the Western European model. Its postwar constitution was drafted by the Allied occupation authorities and adopted by the Diet (parliament) in 1946 under a circumstance that did not permit much open discusssion or opposition. The people was declared "sovereign"; the emperor "shall be the symbol of the State and the unity of the people, deriving his position from the will of the people with whom resides sovereign power" (Article 1). The constitution establishes the legislative supremacy by specifying the Diet as "the highest organ of state power" (Article 41). Although the Supreme Court is empowered "to determine the constitutionality of any law, order, regulation or official act" (Article 81), the Court has repeatedly shown reticence to interfere with the act of the Diet, pointing to the separation of powers stipulated in the constitution.

The Diet consists of two houses. The House of Representatives, or the lower house, has 511 seats which are contested in 124 different constituencies throughout Japan. Members of the lower house are elected to four-year terms which may be terminated if the house is dissolved. The House of Councilors, or the upper house, has a membership of 252, of whom 152 are elected from the 47 prefectures and 100 by the nation at large. The upper-house members are elected for a six-year term, half being elected every three years. The upper house may veto an act of the lower house. To override the veto, a two-third majority of the House of Representatives is required.

The prime minister is elected by the Diet from among its members. The prime minister forms his cabinet, in which the executive power is vested. More than half of the cabinet members must be the members of the Diet. In practice, almost all the cabinet members are selected from among the members of the Diet.

Since 1955 the Liberal Democratic Party (LDP) has been in power. It is a probusiness, pro-American coalition of right-of-center conservatives. Its majority in both houses has steadily eroded in recent elections. The LDP's constituencies are the big and small businesses, and the farmers. The big businesses provide financing to the party and its factions. The LDP has maintained a strong base of electoral power in Japan's agricultural and small business sectors by providing heavy subsidies for rice production and ample financing to small businesses.

The largest opposition party is the Japan Socialist Party (JSP). This party has been in this unenviable position for over a quarter century. It draws much of its support—both in voting and financing—from labor unions and urban industrial workers. Its highly ideological and doctrinaire stance has cost the party heavily in small-business, middle-class, and rural votes. In recent elections, however, the JSP has steadily gained seats in both houses thanks to the continuing trend of urbanization. The Democratic Socialist Party (DSP) is moderately socialistic. It draws its support mainly from the middle-class intellectuals, but has been losing ground steadily in recent elections. Komeito (Clean Government Party) is a political arm of the Buddhist religious organization, Soka Gakkai. The party appeals to the "forgotten people" of Japan—the urban, lower-income, small-business people who are left out of the mainstream of Japanese society. The Japan Communist Party (JCP) is by far the best organized. In order to overcome the stigma attached to communism in Japan, the party has been actively pursuing the "lovable Communist Party" line in recent years.

Japan is divided into 47 prefectures. Prefectural governors and the members of assemblies are locally elected. A prefecture is subdivided into municipalities—local government units consisting of cities, towns, and villages. There are no "unincorporated" areas in a prefecture. Municipalities elect their chiefs and members of their councils. Local autonomy in Japan is highly limited. The prefectures and municipalities have no power to enact laws; they merely establish regulations and by-laws within the framework of the unitary national legal system.

In 1974 there were approximately 4.9 million public employees in Japan, of whom 2.1 million were employed by the national government and the other 2.8 million were employees of local governments. Of the 2.1 million national government employees, 1.2 million were national public servants, and 0.9 million were employees of public enterprises.

A Brief History of Japan[1]

At the beginning of the Christian Era, Japan was controlled by a number of warring clans. By about 400 A.D., the greater part of southwestern Japan came under sway of the Yamato clan. The heads of this clan were the ancestors of the present emperor of Japan. About 550 A.D., Buddhism came to Japan from China, along with the Chinese scripts and Chinese–Buddhist culture, art, and architecture. In the seventh century the country was transformed from a loose federation of clans into a tightly knit monarchical system modeled after the Chinese political system.

In 794 the capital was moved from Nara to Heian-kyo (modern Kyoto) where it remained until 1869. About 1000 A.D. the Japanese culture reached a peak of refinement in Heian-kyo. For the next seven centuries, Japan was ruled by military dictators under a centralized feudal system. Although the emperor still reigned in Kyoto, real power was wielded by warrior aristocrats called *shogun* (hereditary military governor) of the Minamoto, Ashikaga, and Tokugawa families. The 1467–1600 period, known as the Period of Warring Lords (*sengoku jidai*), was an era of chronic strife and civil wars fought by powerful feudal lords vying for the hegemony over the nation.

With the victory at the historic battle of Sekigahara in 1600, Ieyasu Tokugawa unified the entire country, and in 1603 obtained the title of shogun from the emperor. He established his headquarters in Edo (modern

Tokyo) where he laid the foundation of the Tokugawa Shogunate that lasted until 1867.

The Tokugawa *bakufu* (military government) gave Japan 250 years of peace, law, and order, while imposing on the nation total isolation from the rest of the world. This isolation resulted in the remarkable ethnic and cultural homogeneity of the Japanese people. The society did not lay dormant, however. Commercialization and modernization progressed unhindered during this period, paralleling those taking place in the West. By the early 1800s, Edo, with a population of one million, had become the largest city in the world. The nation had central and local governments, and unitary systems of courts and administration. By the end of the Tokugawa period, 30 or 40 percent of the population had received some schooling and acquired rudimentary reading skills. During the period of isolation, however, Japan fell considerably behind the West in the areas of science and technology. The "modernization" of Japan and the rapid growth of the Japanese economy since the 1860s have been essentially a process of bridging the gap between the nation's backward science and technology and its relatively well-developed socioeconomic institutions and cultural refinement.

In 1867 a civil war broke out between the clans loyal to the bakufu and those that advocated restoration of the imperial rule. The bakufu fell, and the imperial restoration was proclaimed by the young emperor Meiji on December 9, 1867. The new imperial Japan immediately launched a determined drive to discard old social and economic order and to replace it with industrialism firmly anchored in modern science and technology. "To catch up with the West" became a national slogan, and the task was to absorb the nation's energy for the next one hundred years.

The character of Japan's expansion was shaped partly by the rampant Western imperialism of the nineteenth century. Fearful of humiliation by the colonial powers and concerned about Japan's survival as a nation and society, the Japanese set out to build a modern industrial state and strong armed forces. *Fukoku kyohei* (rich country, strong military) became a popular slogan. The "strong military" part of the slogan had a few quick pay-offs; Japan's easy victory over China in 1894–95, and the hard-won victory over Czarist Russia in 1904–05 gave the emerging Japanese military clique an unwarranted sense of confidence and a greater desire for more power and influence in Asia. The budding industrialists eagerly collaborated with the military for bigger bites of hapless China.

The United States would never have risked going to war with Japan solely for the sake of rescuing China, and Japan certainly had not wanted to take on America in a hopeless war, but the unfortunate turns of events arising from mutual misunderstanding, ignorance, arrogance, self-righteousness, racial prejudice, and fear drove the two nations to war.[2]

Tension mounted in East Asia as Japan's southward expansion continued, and the breaking point was reached in December 1941.

The defeat in the Pacific War was a deeply traumatic experience for the Japanese. They realized that the *kyohei* (strong military) had failed them. They came to a realization that what mattered the most was economics—the goods, materials, and industrial power. They resumed their long march on the way to catching up with the West, this time with the sole emphasis on *economic* expansion.

The Allied occupation reforms of Japan were sweeping in their nature and coverage. The powerful family-controlled financial cliques, the *zaibatsu,* were dissolved, followed by the enactment of the strong Anti-monopoly Law. Wartime leaders, including a large number of senior bureaucrats, industrialists, and financiers, were purged from public and corporate offices. Unionization of workers created an important new force in the politicoeconomic scene. The sweeping land reform gave land to nearly two million sharecroppers, who provided solid conservative base and a measure of stability in the postwar political situation. The education system was reformed after the American model, with nine years of compulsory education, coeducation of boys and girls, and higher education for the masses.

The outbreak of the Korean War in 1950 caused a drastic about-face in the United States strategy in the Far East. From the "punishment and reform" policy of the late 1940s, the occupation policy shifted to one of building up a strong and prosperous Japan as a close ally of the United States. The occupation of Japan was ended in April 1952. The "special procurement" payments made by the United Nations forces in Japan and Korea—amounting to nearly $4 billion between 1952 and 1956—enabled Japan to reequip her industries. By 1956, Japan's gross national product, both total and per capita, had surpassed the prewar peak level. Under the protection of the U.S. nuclear "umbrella," and with the benefit of the huge U.S. market for its exports, the Japanese economy grew at a phenomenal rate of over 10 percent per year in real terms for the next decade and a half.

In 1968 Japan officially celebrated the centennial of the Meiji Restoration. There was a sense of accomplishment and pride. In the one hundred years, Japan had accomplished the overriding national goal of catching up with the West. The Japanese moved into the 1970s riding the crest of an unprecedented prosperity. Their single-minded pursuit of economic growth and industrial expansion, however, had left them with some very serious social and economic imbalances, notably in the areas of social security, social overhead capital, and environmental safety. Furthermore, the oil crisis of 1973 brought home a valuable lesson—the futility and danger of building an economic supermachine relying almost exclusively on imported resources. By the mid-1970s, a new national consensus began to emerge. The new orientation promises a more moderate and balanced growth, with priorities shifting from heavy industries to "knowledge-intensive" industries. "Balance and maturity" is emerging as a new national slogan.

Notes

1. The standard work in English on the pre-modern history of Japan is the three-volume narrative by Sir George Sansom. George Sansom, *A History of Japan to 1334; A History of Japan, 1334–1615;* and *A History of Japan, 1615–1867* (Stanford, Calif.: Stanford University Press, 1958, 1961, and 1963). See also Edwin O. Reischauer, *Japan, the Story of a Nation* (New York: Alfred A. Knopf, 1970).

2. John Toland, *The Rising Sun: The Decline and Fall of the Japanese Empire 1936–1945* (New York: Random House, 1970), pp. 146–147.

2

The People and Society

Many characteristics of the Japanese economic system are reflections of the character of Japanese social organization which, in turn, is shaped by the nature of the Japanese family. In order to fully understand the Japanese economy, therefore, we must first understand the nature of Japanese society and the Japanese family. For this purpose, however, some knowledge of Japan in the Tokugawa period (1600–1867) is indispensable. The uniquely Japanese familial collectivism and hierarchical social order were nurtured in the Tokugawa incubator for two hundred and fifty years. After more than one hundred years of modernization since the Meiji Restoration, hierarchical familism still strongly conditions the Japanese attitude toward work, government, and society. In fact, contemporary Japanese "capitalism" has more in common with Tokugawa Japan than with today's industrialized socieites of the West.

In this chapter we first examine briefly the main features of the Tokugawa society. We then proceed to study the important elements of contemporary Japanese social life. Specifically, we will see that the patriarchal aspects of the Japanese family account for the status consciousness and hierarchical orientation of Japanese society, and that the hidden matriarchy is related to the group orientation of the Japanese people.

The Tokugawa Legacy

Social Classes and Hierarchy

The overriding objective of the Tokugawa Shogunate was the preservation of the status quo. In order to assure the continued hegemony of the Tokugawa family and the preservation of law and order in the nation, the bakufu government relied heavily on the ideology of Confucianism. Confucius had taught that everyone had a natural station in society. The statuses were hierarchically ordered, and the relationships between them were to be based on benevolence, obedience, and the respect for authority. Consonant with the Confucian ideology, the Japanese society under the Tokugawa regime became highly regimented and hierarchical. The population was divided into four hereditary classes: the warrior-bu-

9

reaucrat (*samurai*), the peasant, the artisan, and the merchant. Strict codes of behavior were prescribed by the bakufu, specifying the manners, clothes that could be worn, and the foods that could be consumed by members of each class. The distinction between the samurai class and the other three, the commoners, was especially pronounced. The samurai was allowed to cut down a member of the lower classes with his sword and leave the scene without further ado when the commoner behaved in an offensive manner to him. The samurai were the governing class. Their duty was loyalty to their master; their occupation was practices of martial arts and learning (Confucian studies).

The distinction between the three commoner classes was less pronounced than that between the samurai and the commoners. Certainly there was no hierarchical ordering among them, although the bakufu meant to place the farmer highest and the merchant lowest. The merchants and artisans were often grouped together as the *chonin* (townspeople) because they normally made a living in towns and cities. Basic literary and computational skills were considered useful for their children. The peasants largely remained illiterate, however, because it was a deliberate policy of the bakufu to keep them ignorant for fear of uprising by enlightened peasants. "Don't let them know" and "Barely keep them alive" were implicit Tokugawa policies toward the peasant population.

In each household, regardless of its class, the hierarchical order and respect for authority were to be strictly observed. The younger siblings were taught to obey their elders. Filial piety was stressed; the wife and the children had to obey and respect the father. Outside the family, the father had to obey the village headman and government officials. Beyond that was the realm of samurai hierarchy. The retainers of a feudal lord (*daimyo*) pledged absolute allegience to the lord. The lord, as a vassal of the shogun, in turn pledged absolute loyalty to the shogun. In harmony with the Confucian ideology, the shogun grudgingly recognized the emperor as the ultimate source of political legitimacy, although the shogun saw to it that the emperor wielded no actual power.

Another downtrodden "class" in Tokugawa Japan was the woman. She was expected to observe "three obediences" in her life: to her parents when a child, to her husband when married, and to her children in her old age. Women and children shared equally low social status. Too much learning was considered undesirable for women, even in the upper-level families. The practice of keeping mistresses was widespread among well-to-do men. The husband could divorce his wife on a variety of grounds by merely informing the wife or her parents in a brief notice called *mikudari-han*, or "three and a half lines."

Rice as the Basis of the Political Economy

The politicoeconomic system of Tokugawa Japan was uniquely tied to the staple foodstuff, rice. Not only was it the basis of the Japanese economy, but was also the material foundation of its fief system. Feudal revenues of the Tokugawa vassals and the stipends of the retainers were expressed, and as a rule were actually paid, in a quantity of rice. At the beginning of the Tokugawa period, the total output of rice in Japan was estimated to be about 24 to 25 million *koku* (of five bushels). By the end of the period, the output had risen to about 35 million koku.[1] The entire country was divided into about 270 fiefs, each ruled by a daimyo who was the head of his clan. The size of a fief was expressed by the number of koku of rice it produced. Thus, a minor daimyo's fief may have produced 10,000 koku of rice, while the largest exceeded one million koku. The daimyo's actual tax yield was about 40 percent of the assessed revenue.

The bakufu directly controlled about a quarter of agricultural land. The feudal revenue was used to support the members of the Tokugawa family and to finance the organization of the central government, which was run by the members, direct vassals, and retainers of the Tokugawa family. The bakufu also directly operated gold and silver mines and controlled the major cities including Edo, Kyoto, and Osaka. The rest of the country was comprised of self-governing fiefs of daimyo, who extracted tax rice from the farmers but paid no taxes to the bakufu. In all, the two million samurai and their families—constituting about 6 to 7 percent of the entire population of about 30 million—appropriated about 40 percent of the total output of the economy.

The Rise of the Merchant Class

Although the daimyo had full control of the people in his territory, and as a matter of right levied taxes on the peasants, the fief was not his property. He had only a grant; therefore, the daimyo could be transferred to another province, or his fief could be confiscated when there was a gross breach of bakufu rules. In such a case, the samurai in the entire clan became *ronin* (masterless samurai) and roamed from province to province seeking new employment. Many a ronin moved to cities and joined street gangs or otherwise lived in dire poverty. Others took refuge in the countryside where they returned to farming.

The bakufu devised many ingenious ways to keep the daimyo under constant control. Bakufu spies infiltrated the provinces, often spending years as ordinary merchants, artisans, or loyal retainers of the daimyo. At times the daimyo were called upon to participate in large-scale construction or development projects which often became heavy financial burdens to them. The system of alternate residence *(sankin kotai)* also proved costly to the daimyo. Under this system, each daimyo was obligated to spend every other year in residence in Edo. He had to leave his wife and children in Edo as de facto hostages to the shogun. The costs of maintaining an official residence in Edo, and of making journeys to and from Edo with a large retinue of samurai in alternate years, were substantial and became heavy drains on the fief finance.

Although initially designed as a political device to keep ambitious vassals under control, the system of sankin kotai produced significant economic consequences. It led to the development of a bourgeois consumption culture in Edo. The population of Edo at the end of the Tokugawa period approached one million, about half of which was samurai and their families and retainers. A large number of artisans and service-related workers were needed to support this large army of nonproductive feudal residents. For the maintenance of the residence in Edo, the daimyo had to ship a large quantity of rice from his province. Consequently, there developed a national market in rice, centering in the strategic seaport city of Osaka. The daimyo either had his rice stored in Osaka warehouses or had it sold there for cash. The warehouses were rented from the Osaka merchants whom the daimyo appointed as administrators. The merchants received a life stipend of rice, with a privilege of assuming a family name and wearing a sword.

Many of these warehouse merchants were also important wholesalers.[2] They imported goods from remote corners of Japan through a string of intermediaries. From the warehouses of the Osaka wholesalers, the goods were shipped by sea to Edo. Osaka thus became the center of commercial activities. Through extension of credit to their customers, many wholesalers developed into merchant bankers. Officially designated by the bakufu as money changers, these merchant bankers engaged in various banking activities such as exchanging different types of specie money and fief currencies, accepting deposits from and extending credit to merchants, clearing accounts of merchants, and discounting bills of exchange. Notes of the larger money changers circulated as money. Thus, besides being the commercial center of the country, Osaka was also the financial center.

The increasing commercialization and monetization of the economy naturally enhanced the prestige and economic power of the merchant class. At the same time, the finance of many a fief became increasingly difficult, partly because of the ineptitude of the fief officials in managing the resources in the province, and partly because of the costly conspicuous consumption in which its Edo household engaged in competition with other daimyo households. Many clans and later the bakufu itself became financially dependent on wealthy merchant houses, and some became heavily indebted to them. By the end of the Tokugawa period, the economic power had gradually shifted to the mercantile class, while the samurai class still enjoyed high status and political power.

The Merchant House[3]

The "house" (*ie*) in the Tokugawa period was a corporate entity that transcended the members of the family. What mattered was the *name* of the house, as it was the embodiment of the achievements and honors of the ancestors. All the members of the house, including its head, were subservient to the name and interest of the house. Although the eldest son of the family as a rule inherited the position of the head of the house, the rule was not always observed. When the eldest son was inept, or when there was no son, a competent young man, either from among the employees or from another merchant house, was adopted as son-in-law. After the retirement of the head, the adopted son would inherit the name traditionally reserved for the head, and assume an autocratic power over the family and the business enterprise.

The employees of the house consisted of apprentices (*detchi*), assistants (*tedai*), and managers (*banto*). The apprentice was recruited, at about age ten or twelve, from other, smaller merchant families or from peasant families. He worked for room and board, but received a small bonus of cash and/or gifts twice a year. At about the age of seventeen or eighteen the apprentice was promoted to assistant. At the age of thirty or over, the assistant could become a manager. Larger houses had more than one manager. The managers and married assistants normally established their own homes nearby and commuted to work. Junior employees lived in the house and often ate in the same kitchen with the younger members of the family. The mistress of the house would look after the welfare of the employees by counseling on their personal problems and even arranging their marriages.

The Tokugawa commercial house was organized as an artificial or simulated kinship group, and the employees were quasi members of the family. As such they enjoyed the benefits of family members. On the other hand, their personal freedom and privacy were highly circumscribed. The characteristics of the Tokugawa employment system—familism, paternalism, lifetime employment, seniority-based reward system, and the lack of privacy for the employees—are still distinctly observed in today's employment relations of large Japanese corporations.

The Village

The great majority (about eight-tenths) of the thirty million Japanese during the Tokugawa period were peasants. With the exception of a small minority of rich farmers and rural industrialists (*sake* and soy brewers and the like), the peasants as a whole lived wretched lives. In many provinces where taxes were high, peasants could not eat the rice they produced. Taxes had to be paid or the penalty was very severe. They subsisted, therefore, largely on coarse grains such as millet or maize.

While the life of the chonin in the cities was relatively easygoing and free of restrictions, the life in the village was highly collectivistic and regimented. Peasants were not allowed to change occupation or leave their land. They could not travel outside of the district without a permit from the authorities. It was vitally important for the feudal class to make sure that a constant and maximum supply of food was forthcoming from the villages. This was made possible by making the work in the field and the delivery of tax produce to the daimyo a collective responsibility of the village. The village headman was charged with the responsibility of assuring the maximum effort on the part of his villagers. Within a village, peasant families were organized into a group of five families (*gonin-gumi*). Again, it was the collective responsibility of the gonin-gumi to complete the necessary work and meet the delivery quota. If one of the families should fall behind in its work, the others had to help it, since the penalty for not meeting the quota would fall on all the five families. In general the obligations of the gonin-gumi were mutual aid and mutual surveillance. Individualism and the independence of spirit naturally did not thrive in such an environment. In a rural community where making a living depended heavily on mutual help and an outsider was treated with hostility, a deviant who invited village ostracism (*mura hachibu*) would soon learn that his survival was threatened.

We now turn to an examination of the characteristics of social organization in contemporary Japan. We will see that the structure of the traditional Japanese family is a basic element in Japanese society.[4]

Patriarchy and Hierarchy

The Family vs. the House

The very core of the traditional Japanese social value is found in the Japanese family system. Other social groups are structured on the pattern of the family, and they share many of its attributes. While the individual is the basic building block of a Western society, the family is the main frame of Japanese society. The three distinguishing characteristics of the Japanese social structure—groupism, hierarchy, and gerontocracy—all have roots in the family. The degree to which every Japanese social organization—be it a company, village, political party, university, or the nation—resembles a family is unparalleled in the industrial world.

It is essential for us to understand at the outset exactly what is meant by the word "family." In a narrow sense, as used in the West, a family is a kinship group, consisting of a couple and its offsprings. In a broader sense, however, family refers to both the kinship group and the collectivity that transcends the individual members, as used in the term "a family estate." It is in the latter, broader sense that the word "family" is often used in discussions of Japanese social organization. In contrast, the Japanese concept of the "house" (*ie*) is even broader; it refers to the family collectivity, the family line, including both the living and the dead. In what follows, the word "family" will be used interchangeably with the word "house" (*ie*).

Traditionally, the house has been the predominant frame of reference in Japanese kinship relations. The concept of a nuclear family has become established only in recent decades. Even today, the house takes precedence over the biological family in more traditional, well-established families. The Japanese house has a life of its own. It was founded by its ancestors and has been passed onto its present incumbents. The members do not constitute the house; they merely belong to it and are subjacent to it. The collectivity is basic; the individual is secondary. When the eldest son takes a bride, the pattern is that of "Miss Suzuki joining the House of Honda," rather than "John marrying Jane."

Although the postwar Civil Code no longer recognizes the house as a legal institution, the practice in most propertied families is to let the house inherit the property under the custody of the eldest son. The law can be circumvented by either the elder relatives pressuring the younger children to sign away their shares of the property, or by simply ignoring the law. As a rule, the collective pressure and the individuals' apprehension of disrupting the group harmony combine to create a mood of circumspection and acquiescence on the part of the victims.

Authority in the Family

In the old Japan, the tradition and the law required that the members of the house obey the father. The wife and children had no concept of rights, only of duties. Parental power was exercised by the father, while the mother assisted him in the task. This tradition of male dominance is clearly not consonant with the reality in today's Japan. One even hears about the matriarchal nature of the Japanese family. How is the authority in the family exercised? What are the roles of its members? The answers to these questions reveal a great deal about Japanese society and its people.

The authority relationship in most families is as follows: The father is the head of the family; patriarchy is assumed or pretended. Socially, the husband's status is superior to that of his wife. He usually calls his wife and children by their first names, whereas it is not proper for them to reciprocate. In public, the wife refers to her husband as her *shujin* (literally, master), while the husband refers to her as his *kanai* (literally, "inside the house").

The status of each family member is rigidly fixed in a hierarchical order—the father at the top and the youngest daughter at the bottom. The younger children must defer to their parents and to the older children in strict accordance with their ages, both in manner and speech. The precedence of elder over younger is a deeply ingrained Confucian moral ethic, and not even a very "modern" family nowadays can be completely free of it. Even twins are ranked according to the exact time of their births. Unless the twins' elder–younger distinction is made, their births cannot be recorded at the city hall. Tradition-sensitive parents teach the junior twin to defer to the senior twin in language and demeanor.

The traditional Japanese family is the prototype of Japanese social organization; there is a clearly distinguishable hierarchy of status, there are no persons of equal ranks, and there is, as a rule, a perfect parallel between the hierarchies of status and age. All of these characteristics are reflected more or less in Japanese social organization. For example, the emphasis on age (gerontocracy) in Japanese society is attributed to the fact that, in a family, age and status are correlated. Authority grows and status rises with age progression. The Japanese have an innate desire to preserve this parallel in their social organization.

Ranking Consciousness

The vertical orientation of the Japanese family is a central integrative principle of Japanese social organization. Persons seldom relate to each other as equals; they exhibit a marked propensity to place themselves in a hierarchical order. Three broad types of vertical relation can be identified in large-scale formal organizations.

The Superior–Subordinate Relation. In a bureaucratic organization, the ranking is explicitly a function of the positions or titles assumed by individuals. The subordinate bolsters the superior's authority (and ego) by the use of deferential demeanor and language. The subordinate should avoid an open confrontation with his superior. When there is a conflict of opinion or interest, the subordinate must always defer to his superior. It is customary for the subordinate to pay the superior periodical visits and to present him with seasonal gifts.

The *Senpai–Kohai* Relation. The senior–junior relation in an organization is based on seniority. All members of a group are divided into three categories: *senpai* (senior), *kohai* (junior) and *dohai*. Dohai are persons of equal seniority. The senpai–dohai–kohai relationship is couched in terms of a time-sequence framework. Persons who joined the organization earlier are one's senpai. Thus, to a college sophomore, juniors and seniors are his senpai, other sophomores are his dohai, and freshmen are kohai. A kohai is naturally expected to show an attitude of deference and circumspection to his senpai.

The concept of *seniority* used in describing the senpai–kohai relation needs a few words of explanation. Seniority means more than the length of service; in a typical Japanese social organization, it translates directly into rank and, very likely, also age. A senpai tends to be older and higher ranking than his kohai. Furthermore, senpai–kohai relations are observed only within a same status group. A young managerial employee, for example, does not consider an older blue-collar worker as his senpai no matter how long the latter has been working in the same company. One's senpai is essentially a person who is more advanced than he is in seniority, rank, and perhaps in age in the same line of work or endeavor.

The *Oyabun–Kobun* Relation. In an organization there may develop an *oyabun–kobun* relation, which can be loosely translated as patron–protégé or leader–follower relation. This relationship is particularly personal and emotive, and may grow out of either superior–subordinate or senpai–kohai relation. Basically, the relationship is one of protection and loyalty similar in nature to the feudal lord–vassal relation or the modern gangleader–gangster relation.[a]

In society at large, individuals are ranked according to their status, age, sex, etc., status being the most important criterion. (Professor Nakane observes that in American society sex-consciousness predominates over status-consciousness.[5] In fact, to an uninitiated Japanese it appears odd to observe an American male of superior status deferring, in

---

[a]The senpai–kohai and oyabun–kobun relations will be discussed further in a subsequent section.

a social situation, to a female of lower status.) In their social relations, the Japanese cannot escape from ranking consciousness. It is difficult for them to carry on a conversation with strangers without knowing the relative ranks of the persons involved, just as one cannot refer to a third person in English unless one knows that person's sex (the "he or she" problem). Except for the "buddy talks" used among siblings, classmates, and intimate coworkers, there is no neutral-level spoken Japanese. Whenever the Japanese meets a stranger, therefore, he instinctively ranks the stranger relative to himself so that an appropriate level of honorifics (*keigo*) may be used.[6]

The rank consciousness of the Japanese is extended to nonpersonal relations. Firms, schools, government agencies and other organizations are ranked in the popular mind. It is a matter of vital concern for the workers of a corporation to know where their firm stands within the industry. Within a corporation, departments and sections are ranked according to their importance and prestige. Even nations are ranked, gross national product being the most often used criterion in this ranking. In international relations, Japan tends to be agreeable and accommodating to higher-ranking nations and aggressive or contemptuous of lower-ranking countries.

Hierarchy, Continuity, and National Identity

The Japanese house is not necessarily a blood stream, but it is definitely a name flow that continues through time. Every eldest Japanese boy realizes that he stands in a line of descent from his remote ancestors, and, like his father, he will one day become the head of the house and take up the responsibility of assuring its prosperity and continuity. The younger sons can also claim collateral lineage when they split off from the main house (*honke*) and establish branch houses (*bunke*). As electricity flows to branch circuits, the name of the house flows to all branch houses. When a man marries into another house as son-in-law and assumes its name, he inherits the time continuity of that house. What matters is the name, not the blood.

The branch house is naturally subordinate to the main house from which it derives its legitimacy. The head of a branch house pays respects to the head of the main house on festive occasions. In a rural village, many families share the same family name and lineage. The honke–bunke relation is observed in a strictly hierarchical order, and the members of the main house enjoy considerable prestige. They may even interfere, as a matter of right, with the internal affairs of a branch household.

The institution of the house leaves a strong imprint on the character of Japanese society; it establishes, at the same time, a hierarchical order and time continuity. Since the house continues through time by means of branching, we can theoretically trace any family tree all the way back, through a succession of branch–main linkages, to the ultimate main house. The present imperial family is presumably the direct descendant of the original main house. Thus, to the Japanese, the emperor is not just another king. He is the head of the honke of all the *honke* (main houses) in Japan. He is in popular belief the direct primogenitary descendant of the ancestors of all Japanese—the mythical gods and goddesses of ancient Japan. By the logical extension of the superior–subordinate relationship between main and branch houses, the Japanese attribute an infinitely high rank to the emperor because he is the pinnacle of the hierarchy of families. Japan is one big family, with the emperor as its paterfamilias and high priest. He is the ultimate source of legitimacy, and as such, accords legitimacy to the entire hierarchical order of Japanese society. The Japanese derive their keen sense of national identity and continuity from the familial nature of their nation.

The Public vs. the Private

It has been said that in Japan the public takes precedence over the private; the private is subordinate to the official. This orientation is closely related to the institution of the house and the hierarchical social order.[7]

In English, "public" connotes commonality, and "private" implies self-interest and individual dignity. The Japanese term for "public" (*ko* or *oyake*) and for "private" (*shi* or *watakushi*) have meanings quite different from their English equivalents. The original meaning of the word *oyake* was probably "great house," that is, a main house in the village. The branch house, or more specifically, the head of the branch house, was *watakushi* to oyake. Consequently, there are strong overtones of the subordinate position of the private in relation to the public. At each level of the national family tree, the head of a house acted simultaneously as oyake to his branch houses and watakushi to those above him. The emperor, being the head of the honke of all honke, was watakushi only to his ancestors.

Thus, oyake came to mean authority from above (the "public," the state, the officialdom), and watakushi came to mean subordination to authority (the "private," the self). To the average Japanese, therefore, the term "public servant" seems, even today, somewhat of a contradiction in terms. A government official represents the higher authority of the state (if not of the emperor) and therefore must be obeyed by the "private" citizens. The age-old tradition of *kanson minpi* (officialdom revered, people disdained) has its roots in the Japanese concept of "public" and "private."

Matriarchy and Groupism

We have thus far examined the patriarchal aspects of the Japanese family and their imprints on society—the status and rank consciousness and hierarchy orientation. We now turn to consider the other important dimension of the Japanese family—the matriarchal orientation, and the groupism which is nurtured by it.

Japan was a matriarchy in its early days.[8] The sun goddess Amaterasu-Omikami was the legendary founder of the imperial family line. The oldest Chinese account of Japan described it as a country ruled by a queen. Until the ninth century, men moved to their wives' homes after marriage. The importation of Confucianism from China, however, brought patriarchal ideology to Japan. It was quickly adopted by the Japan of "warring lords," and by the fifteenth century it had been firmly established.

The Need to Belong to a Group

One of the most outstanding characteristics of Japanese society is the importance of groups. Most Japanese feel secure only if they belong to a group and are totally accepted by it. The Japanese would feel lost if he had no place in a group, much as a child would without a place in a family. It is well recognized that this emotional need of the Japanese to depend on a group has its roots in the child-rearing practices and socialization process—the relation between the mother and the child.[9] In the society dominated by men, the Japanese wife tends to retreat to the home and build her own cocoon there. Her husband is likely to have a social life of his own outside of the home, primarily with his coworkers. A husband's evening out in town does not, as a rule, include the wife, nor is the custom of socializing with other couples widespread. When the first baby arrives, therefore, the wife is prepared to devote herself totally to it. A Japanese home with young children revolves around the mother-and-child relationship; the husband becomes an appendage.

A Japanese baby is born into a situation almost exclusively designed to provide him nurturance and protection. The mother is totally devoted to the task of meeting the baby's needs and satisfying its whims. She never lets the baby cry for long; she picks it up and rocks him patiently until he stops crying or falls asleep. Besides feeling guilty herself, the mother must worry about the critical ear of her relatives (especially her mother-in-law) and neighbors. To the Japanese mother, the Western practice of putting the baby to its own bed and letting him cry himself to sleep seems bordering on cruelty. Vogel reports that one Japanese mother, after seeing an American movie, said that she felt sorry for the "poor foreign babies" who were forced to sleep alone.[10] In most Japanese homes a baby does not have its own room. The mother sleeps and bathes with the baby. Consequently, there is constant body contact between them. As the baby grows, the mother spends an inordinate amount of time with him; it becomes the focal point of her life.

This physical and emotional closeness between the mother and her child appears to be the basic cause of the Japanese adult's craving for dependence: he remembers the sense of warmth and total protection of his childhood and longs to duplicate it in his adult social life. The Japanese men who run the male-dominated society are in fact a number of adolescents who eternally yearn for the warmth of the Great Mother. In many homes the wife becomes a substitute mother, and the husband becomes the "biggest boy" in the family. (For some men, bar hostesses become substitute mothers.) The old matriarchy thus reemerges. The position of the woman in Japanese society is thus stronger than meets the eye.

The dependency need of the people can be satisfied by their belonging to a group—not just any group, but a group organized on a familial pattern—from which they can draw a sense of belonging and security. Most Japanese secondary groups therefore have strong familial overtones. The group is likely to (1) have a particularistic membership and be closed to outsiders; (2) allow a member to make an emotional commitment to it, but expect him to play his assigned role faithfully in the interest of the group; and (3) allow the member to grow in stature and authority as he grows older without too much competition within the group.

Membership in a Japanese social organization is basically particularistic. (Membership is said to be "particularistic" when the criteria for selection are not germane to the position, and "universalistic" when the position can be defined by certain objective criteria and can be filled by any individual who satisfy the criteria.) A sharp distinction is made between the insiders (us, the family members) and the outsiders (them, the strangers), the latter being met with indifference or even hostility by the former. Just as a person is born into a family, a new member is allowed to enter an organization, as a rule, only at the bottom of the hierarchy. Entry at any other level would disrupt the delicate balance between the seniority, age, and authority of the existing members in the hierarchy. This is why government agencies and large corporations recruit employees once a year only from among the year's new graduates.

Status Quo

One is not supposed to move around from job to job or from college to college, just as he does not move around from family to family in his life. Normally, therefore, a worker stays in a company throughout his career, and universities do not accept credit from other universities. A midcareer recruit of a company, a transfer student in a high school, and a foreigner living in Japan for a number of years, all share a common frustrating sense of not being totally accepted. For similar reasons, the Japanese who graduates from a university abroad cannot expect to get into the mainstream of Japanese society, unless he first secured a place in a Japanese organization and then studied abroad on a leave-of-absence basis.

The Japanese social structure consists of countless cul-de-sacs. People enter them early in life and stay there for life. There is very little communication between the individual members and the outside world. Inside each cul-de-sac, the residents are related to each other vertically, and their total emotional participation generates a sense of unity and *en* (bond, karma). The individual members are related to society by their group membership. Thus, a person is a Mitsubishi employee first (group identity), section chief second (status in a group), and an accountant third (profession). A significant corollary of group consciousness, therefore, is the lack of profession or class consciousness. The relationship among accountants belonging to different groups is remote and impersonal; there is no familial relation. The same is true with the proletariat: they do not form a familial group, hence there is no *en* among them. Stratification is not a characteristic of Japanese society: it cannot be sliced horizontally into strata. The organization principle is a vertical splitting implied in hierarchical groupism.

Submerged in a group

Emotional Participation in a Group

The Japanese becomes totally submerged in a group. He identifies his achievements with the success of his shop, his section, his company, and his country. He finds an opportunity for personal fulfillment in the group. The status and rank consciousness of the Japanese now emerges as consciousness of ranking or rating of one's group. Within an industry, for example, the rating of a company becomes a matter of vital concern for the employees of the company. They also exhibit keen sensitivity to the relative rating of their section within the company. A strong sense of camaraderie and unity develops within the group, the emotive content of which serves to satisfy the psychological needs of the members.

The emotional participation of a Japanese in a group goes far to explain certain uniquely Japanese phenomena. It explains, first, why the Japanese workers prefer to become involved in a multiplicity of mutual activities at their places of work, and like to socialize with their co-workers after the working hours. Second, it helps to explain the Japanese obsession with maintaining a harmonious relationship, *wa,* within the group. This preoccupation with harmony in turn explains their tendency to seek consensus and compromises, and their dislike of an adversary system, confrontation, and the majority rule. Third, the emotive content of group participation makes a stigma of group contempt so much more unbearable. Consequently, the individual group member endeavors to live up to the role expected of him by the group.

Hirschmeier and Yui call this aspect of Japanese ethics "functional role expectation" because "the Japanese feels a deep urge to satisfy the expectations as internal imperative."[11] Ruth Benedict argued that Japanese ethics was "shame ethics," in which the fear of being ridiculed and rejected by others constituted a major moral sanction.[12] This fear is no doubt inculcated in the child's mind by his mother constantly admonishing him not to do things that might make other people laugh at him, thereby bringing shame to the family. George De Vos has maintained that Japan is a guilt-culture, based on the guilt a person feels when he fails to meet social expectations and thereby hurts his mother.[13] It seems to make little difference whether we call this aspect of Japanese ethics guilt, shame, or functional role expectation. For our purposes it suffices to say that the basic driving force of the Japanese people is derived from their group orientation and dependency.

Debts and Obligations

Interpersonal debts and obligations are observable in any society. Three such obligational relationships are identifiable in Japanese society: *kari, giri,* and *on. Kari* (debt) is a simple sense of indebtedness arising from some act of benevolence on the part of another person. For example, one might owe his friend a treat to a dinner at a restaurant or assistance in moving furniture. When an American couple talks about owing some other couple a party or a dinner, they mean exactly the kari debt. The essence of the kari relation is that it can be easily repaid. If you owe your friend a party, invite him over to your party and the book is cleared.

Giri (social obligation) is the whole sweep of human obligational relationships dictated by tradition—duties people must fulfill as members of closely knit communities. While a kari relationship may arise between individuals who are mere acquaintances, giri relations can exist only between persons who are particularistically related to each other. The nature of this relationship determines the intensity of the attendant giri obligation. One feels a sense of giri to his senpai, oyabun, senior relatives and in-laws, and superiors at his place of work. The closer the relationship, the more intense is the obligation. There are no specific deeds one must perform to fulfill one's giri obligations, except that one must not neglect sending seasons' greetings and attending weddings and funerals. More generally, a person who is under a giri obligation is expected to stand ready to assist those to whom he owes the obligation: the essence of the obligation is that he cannot say no when he is asked for a favor or assistance. One refuses to fulfill giri obligations at the risk of being stigmatized as a *girishirazu* (an ingrate; literally "a person who knows no giri").

On (eternal gratitude) is a sense of gratitude one is expected to feel toward others for a great deed of kindness or favor rendered to him. *On* favor is considered infinite; that is, it is so great that it can never be repaid. One is expected to feel *on* sense of gratitude to his parents, and persons who gave him unusual "breaks" in his life or career. A person who saves your life, rescues you from a financial disaster, or discovers you and launches you to a successful career becomes your lifetime *onjin* (*on*-benefactor).

Of the three obligational relationships discussed above, giri is by far the most potent social force. Kari relations are short-lived, and *on* relations are few and far between. In contrast, giri relationships are conterminous with Japanese social relations. Even in and between formal social organizations, such as private corporations and government offices, giri considerations, working through senpai–kohai and oyabun–kobun relations, generate unique Japanese social dynamics.

The Amae *Syndrome*

Earlier in this chapter we observed the hierarchy orientation of Japanese society and social organization. We then saw that the Japanese have a keenly felt need for dependency on a group. There appears to exist a conflict between the two: hierarchy and dependency. How could the Japanese derive emotional fulfillment from a group that is organized on a hierarchical principle which implies authority and impersonality? The answer, again, lies in the familial nature of Japanese organization; specifically, the close personal ties between superior and subordinate and the special quality of dependency. If a child can fulfill his emotional needs from his dependency on the family without resenting the family hierarchy and the authority of the parents, so could a member of an organization. Chie Nakane argues that the basic structural principle of Japanese society is the relationship between two individuals of upper and lower status.[14]

In any situation involving vertical personal relations (e.g., foreman–

worker, professor–student, parent–child), the Japanese instinctively develop a very intense dependency relationship. What is the quality of this relationship? Dr. Takeo Doi, a noted Japanese psychiatrist, introduced an interesting hypothesis centering upon the concept of *amae*.[15] The verb *amaeru,* to which there is no equivalent in Western languages, is derived from the adjective *amai* (sweet), and means "to depend and presume upon one's superior's affection" or "to bask in one's superior's indulgence." The subordinate (or junior) presumes upon the personal affection of his superior (or senior) and expects him to provide protection, just as a child presumes upon his parents' love and protection. The superior accepts this presumption, allows a certain amount of indulgence, and generally takes care of the subordinate's emotional needs. The superior himself, of course, draws a certain amount of gratification from the situation. In turn, also, the superior amaeru on his own superior. This subtle but pervasive dependency relationship between superior (senior) and subordinate (junior) serves as a powerful reinforcement to the familial hierarchy of Japanese social organization.

The Clique

Japanese society is replete with various types of cliques (*batsu*) structured on the vertical principle. There are *habatsu* (factional cliques, especially in bureaucratic organizations and political parties), *zaibatsu* (financial cliques), *keibatsu* (kinship cliques), *gakubatsu* (university cliques) and *kyodobatsu* (home province cliques). Most cliques are organized on the oyabun–kobun and/or senpai–kohai principle.

The oyabun–kobun relation is basically a parent–child relationship. (*Oya* means parent, *ko* means child, and *bun* means status.) In an organization, a superior (not necessarily an immediate superior) or a senpai may take an early interest in a particular subordinate or kohai. If the junior reciprocates the feeling—that is, if he feels that the particular senior is worthy of his respect and affection and/or if he feels the superior would be useful in his advancement in the organization—then an oyabun–kobun relation is formed. It is usually a very subtle relationship, except in the gangleader–gangster relation, in which the relationship is openly recognized by all concerned and the words oyabun and kobun are actually used. Perhaps because of the gangland connotation, most oyabun–kobun partners would be embarassed or irked if someone referred to them, in their presence, as oyabun and kobun.

The senpai–kohai (senior–junior) relation is less personal and involves less emotional commitment than the oyabun–kobun relation. It is more like the big brother–little brother relationship than the parent–child

relationship. In a bureaucratic organization, one may find among his superiors a number of senpai from his own university or from the same province. Whether or not he develops an oyabun–kobun relation with one of them, the advantage of his being a member of a gakubatsu (university clique) or a kyodobatsu (home province clique) is substantial, since a number of senpai naturally take interest in him simply because he is their kohai (little brother).

The clique is so pervasive in Japanese government, corporate, and academic organizations that one cannot expect to function effectively, let alone advance rapidly, without the benefit of one sort of clique or another. Many clique relations, moreover, extend beyond the boundaries of particular organizations. For example, the Tokyo University clique in government, industry, and academia forms a formidable elite power group. Similarly, a retired high government official who heads a private firm can count on special assistance from the members of his clique in the old ministry.

Horizontal Bonds of Equality

Considering that Japanese social relations are projections of the Japanese family where everybody is ranked, we might conclude that it is impossible for the Japanese to experience an interpersonal relation that is totally free of ranking. This, however, is not the case. A group of individuals can be "born" into a social organization *simultaneously* and thereby become its members with an equal rank. This happens when a group of young people enroll in a school or university as freshmen, or when a group of new graduates enter a firm or government office as new recruits. In such cases, no ranking can be established within the group. To the Japanese who must constantly be conscious of ranks, egalitarian relationship found among *dohai* or *dokyusei* (classmates) is a welcome relief. Deep and long-lasting friendships often develop out of such relationships. This curious vacuum of equality that exists in the nodes of the hierarchical Japanese social order is held dear by the participants. Within the larger framework of vertical ties, the horizontal bonds uniting persons of an equal rank serve as an important, albeit secondary, integrative force. It must be remembered, however, that "equality" here means that a group of individuals are *equally* inferior or superior to some other groups in an organization. It is a far cry from the equality of individuals as understood in the West.

Notes

1. George Sansom, *A History of Japan, 1615–1867* (Stanford, Calif.: Stanford University Press, 1963), p. 4.

2. For an excellent discussion of the merchants in Tokugawa Japan, see: Johannes Hirschmeier and Tsunehiko Yui, *The Development of Japanese Business 1600–1973* (Cambridge, Mass.: Harvard University Press, 1975), chap. 1.

3. Discussions in this subsection are drawn largely from ibid., pp. 38–43.

4. For excellent discussions of the Japanese people and society, see: Frank Gibney, *Japan: The Fragile Superpower* (New York: W. W. Norton, 1975); Chie Nakane, *Japanese Society* (Berkeley and Los Angeles: University of California Press, 1972); Ezra Vogel, *Japan's New Middle Class: The Salary Man and His Family in a Tokyo Suburb* (Berkeley and Los Angeles: University of California Press, 1963); and William H. Forbis, *Japan Today: People, Places, Power* (New York: Harper and Row, 1975).

5. Chie Nakane, *Japanese Society,* p. 32.

6. For a discussion of *keigo,* see: Roy Andrew Miller, "Levels of Speech (*keigo*) and the Japanese Response to Modernization," in Donald H. Shively, ed., *Tradition and Modernization in Japanese Culture* (Princeton, N J.: Princeton University Press, 1971), chap. XV.

7. The following discussion draws upon J. Victor Koschmann, "The Idioms of Contemporary Japan X: *Ko to Shi,*" *Japan Interpreter* 9 (Winter 1975): 361–367.

8. See Gibney, *Japan,* pp. 134–143 for an interesting account of Japan's "hidden matriarchy."

9. For a detailed account of Japanese child rearing, see Vogel, *Japan's New Middle Class,* chap. XII.

10. Ibid., p. 231.

11. Hirschmeier and Yui, Development of Japanese Business, p. 52.

12. Ruth Benedict, *The Chrysanthemum and the Sword: Patterns of Japanese Culture* (Boston: Houghton Mifflin Co., 1946), pp. 222–227.

13. Geroge A. De Vos, *Socialization for Achievement: Essays on the Cultural Psychology of the Japanese* (Berkeley and Los Angeles: University of California Press, 1973), reviewed by J. Victor Koschmann and Nancy Lee Koschmann, "What Makes the Japanese 'Japanese'," *Japan Interpreter* 9 (Summer-Autumn 1974): 239.

14. Nakane, *Japanese Society,* p. 42.

15. Takeo Doi, *Amae no Kozo* [The structure of amae] (Tokyo: Kobunsha, 1971). For a fairly extensive discussion of amae in Japanese society, see Gibney, *Japan,* chap. VI.

3

The Educational System and Occupational Allocation

A Particularistic Meritocracy

We observed in the preceding chapter that membership in a Japanese social organization is basically particularistic. A person must be "born" into an organization, not just "move" into it from the outside, in order to be totally accepted by other members as one of their kind. This is true with most large, formal organizations, including business corporations and government offices. The larger, the more important, and the more prestigious the organizations are, the more pronounced is their particularistic tendency.

Positions in organizations, however, are not given on the basis of *ascriptive* characteristics of individuals such as kinship, caste, or father's social status. Rather, entrance is based on *achieved* characteristics, primarily of schooling. Again, these tendencies are more pronounced the larger and the more prestigious the organizations are. In a small family-operated business firm, in contrast, kinship connections may be more important considerations than education in accepting employees.

Two opposing views are possible concerning the Japanese system of occupational allocation. One sees it primarily as an achievement-oriented system. Unlike the traditional societies (and to some extent the Western European societies), occupational selection in Japan, at least outside the small business and farming sectors, is not by particularistic considerations. The son of a poor peasant can advance to a very high level through sheer competence. His father's occupation, wealth, social status, or connections are of little consequence if he is bright and industrious.

An opposite view is also possible. A person is given only one chance in his lifetime, at about age eighteen, to compete for an entry into the mainstream of Japanese society—the corporate and government sectors. If he fails, he will be denied a second chance, regardless of his individual qualities. He will be treated as a second-class citizen and excluded from "the place in the sun," unless he succeeds in the fields of sports, entertainment, or arts. Occupational tracks are ranked in a well recognized hierarchy of prestige, reward, and power. Which track an individual is allowed to follow is determined by the extent and quality of his educational career. Once he enters a track in his youth, moving to a higher level track is extremely difficult, if not impossible. Even in the world of government agencies and large corporations, there are many different levels

29

of career tracks, and which level one is allowed to enter is again largely a function of the extent and quality of his schooling. In this view, then, Japan is definitely not meritocratic.

Paradoxically, both views are essentially accurate reflections of the unique Japanese system of particularistic meritocracy. To put it simply, the requirement of economic rationality is met by stressing merit before occupations are allocated; after that, particularistic considerations become paramount. The basic value orientation of society is thereby preserved. Those who enter a Japanese social organization at the bottom of its hierarchy are "born" into the organizational family. Instead of birth ascription, Japanese society allows a second-chance ascription by educational achievement. Entry into a firm or government office is a "kind of rebirth, a process of permanent reascription in terms of achievement up to that date."[1]

The Educational System

Like the United States and the Soviet Union, Japan is a mass education society.[2] In the early 1970s, one out of five Japanese was in school. A total of nine years of schooling is compulsory: six years of elementary school and three years of middle school. Kindergarten and high schools (three years beyond the middle school) are not compulsory, but attendance is becoming nearly universal. In 1974, 92 percent of middle school graduates proceeded to high schools. Higher education consists of junior colleges (two years) and four-year universities. Of the 410 universities that existed in 1974, eighty were national universities, thirty-two were public (prefectural and municipal) universities, and the remaining 298 were private institutions. The proportion of students enrolled in private universities was 78 percent; in private junior colleges, 91 percent.[3] In 1975 there were 428 universities with 1,734,000 students and 513 junior colleges with 354,000 students. Twenty-one percent of university students and 86 percent of junior college students were women. The total number of college and university students exceeded one million in 1965 and two million in 1975.[4] The percentage of college age population attending colleges and universities increased from 10 percent in 1960 to 30 percent in 1975.[5] In 1974, sixty-three national, nineteen public, and 121 private universities offered graduate programs. There were 32,030 students enrolled in master's degree programs, and 14,835 students were in doctorate programs.[6]

The Occupational Horizon

The occupational horizon of the great majority of the Japanese is almost exclusively determined by the highest level of schooling they attain, and, in cases of university graduates, which university they graduate from. Again, what matters is group identity. A graduate of the University of Tokyo is identified with that institution; what he studied there, how well he did, or what degree he received—these are relatively unimportant attributes of the all important group identity.

Typical ranges of occupations predetermined by the levels of schooling are as follows:[a]

Middle Schools:
    Farming, trades, and services
    Small and medium-sized firms, blue collar
    Small and medium-sized firms, clerical
    Large corporations, blue collar*
High Schools:
    Farming, trades, and services
    Small and medium-sized firms, blue collar
    Small and medium-sized firms, clerical–administrative
    Large corporations, blue collar*
    Large corporations, clerical*
    National and local governments, clerical*
Universities:
    Professions
    Small and medium-sized firms, administrative
    Less prestigious large corporations, administrative*
    Local governments, administrative*
    National government, administrative (noncareer)*
Elite Universities:
    Professions
    Large corporations, administrative*
    Local governments, administrative*
    National government, administrative (noncareer and career)*

The occupational horizon of the middle school graduate is limited largely to farming, trades, services, and small businesses. Middle school graduates who are hired by large corporations are mostly girls to perform simple tasks on assembly lines. The high school graduate can find employment in government or large corporations, but he cannot, as a rule, expect to rise above the lower middle management level. In general, high school graduates fill blue collar and clerical jobs. In government and corporate bureaucracies, their status and opportunities are akin to those of noncommissioned officers in the military services. Graduates of col-

---

[a]An asterisk indicates that formal entrance examinations are required. See Chapter 4 for the difference between career and noncareer administrators in the national government.

leges and universities are *eligible* to enter government offices and large corporations. The better and more prestigious their schools are, the more *qualified* they are for jobs in larger and more prestigious corporations and government agencies. Actual placements depend on the results of competitive examinations and interviews given to qualified candidates.

About 10 percent of the Japanese youth seeking college entrance succeed in entering a dozen or so of the most prestigious, "elite" universities.[b] Major corporations vie for the better graduates of these universities. The largest and most prestigious corporations recruit only from the best few of these institutions. The recruits from these universities are treated differently from others in training and promotion. Their position is comparable to the service academy graduates in the U.S. military services. The graduates of the elite universities also tend to do much better than the graduates of ordinary universities in civil service examinations. Consequently, the government bureaucracy has a disproportionately large share of these graduates, particularly at the higher ranks.

Especially conspicuous is the influence wielded by the graduates of the University of Tokyo in business, government, politics, and higher education. According to one study, 41 percent of prominent business leaders were Tokyo graduates.[7] National government bureaucracy is a traditional stronghold of Tokyo men. In the 1950s, 79 percent of career bureaucrats (section chief up to vice-minister) were Tokyo University graduates. Five other state universities supplied 13 percent, and all the private universities combined accounted for only 3 percent. In the 1960s, the percentages of Tokyo graduates among section chiefs and higher officials (excluding vice-ministers) ranged from 53 percent in the Transportation Ministry to 73 percent in the Local Autonomy Ministry.[8] Comparable studies show that George Washington University supplied the largest group (3 percent) of the U.S. federal career civil service executives in 1959, while Oxford and Cambridge graduates in 1950 accounted for 47 percent of British civil servants with the rank of assistant secretary or above.[9]

As discussed earlier, occupational allocation in Japan has a strong overtone of ascription—a reascription by education early in one's life. The crucial point comes at about age eighteen. At this point a youth must decide whether or not he goes to a university. For a high school graduate who is in the upper half of his class academically, it is not difficult to enter a university provided that he is not choosy about which university he attends or his family is wealthy enough to afford the very high tuition

---

[b]Seven former Imperial Universities, including Tokyo and Kyoto; plus Hitotsubashi University; Kobe University; and the two best private universities, Keio and Waseda. The top three are Tokyo, Kyoto, and Hitotsubashi.

fees of a private university. The national and other public (municipal and prefectural) universities are harder to get into, although their tuition fees are modest. Entrance examinations to the elite universities are very competitive, and only the brightest and most industrious high school graduates with years of preparation succeed in the entrance examinations to the most prestigious national universities such as Tokyo, Kyoto, and Hitotsubashi. Social selection is made essentially at age eighteen, since once the youth is admitted to a university he is not likely to fail. Attendance requirements and standards for grades are lax in most universities. The university officials and faculty regard their students with paternalistic attitude; the fact that they succeeded in the ruthless entrance examinations is considered a good enough guarantee of their worth. The students are therefore seldom dismissed for academic reasons. The university keeps them for four years, graduates them, and does its best to find employment for its "children." Unlike American university students who must study hard after they enter college, Japanese students must study *before* they are admitted, but can relax afterwards.

The Examination Hell

Because of the importance of entering the right university, preparations for college entrance examinations become an all-absorbing factor in the lives of the more ambitious precollege youth. This national obsession with examinations creates a pathological phenomenon known in Japan as *shiken jigoku* (examination hell).[10]

A popular strategy for enhancing one's chance of getting into a "good" university is to enter a high school, public or private, that has an excellent record of placing a large number of graduates in the first-class universities. Since the University of Tokyo is the most prestigious school and the most difficult one to get into, the number of graduates a high school places in a given year in that university is used as an indicator of the "excellence" of that high school. In recent years, Nada High School in Hyogo Prefecture has led the list of the most successful high schools, placing somewhere between 120 and 150 graduates in Tokyo University every year out of a graduating class of about 220 students.[11] We can easily see how extraordinary these figures are when we consider that there are close to 5,000 high schools in Japan, and Tokyo University accepts about 3,000 freshmen each year. Nada is a private, six-year school combining middle and high schools. It covers the curricula of middle and high schools in five years and devotes the sixth year exclusively to preparations for college examinations. It is no exaggeration to say that the paramount goal of Nada education is to raise its "Tokyo University entrance ratio.'' Students are constantly drilled on mock college entrance examinations. Little time is wasted on sports or extracurricular activities. The reputation of the school has in turn made it a prestigious school that is difficult to get into. Fifth and sixth grade pupils in the Osaka–Kobe area schools spend afternoons and evenings at private preparatory schools studying for the entrance examinations to Nada Middle School.[12]

Konaka describes the life of one Nada High School sophomore. The boy lives in a one-room efficiency apartment rented by his family which lives in a remote province. Every day after school the boy studies between three and five in the afternoon. He eats supper in the cafeteria in the apartment building; afterwards, he sleeps between 7 P.M. and midnight. Getting up at midnight, he studies until seven in the morning. At seven-thirty, he leaves for school. There is no radio or television set in his room. No novels and other "unnecessary" books are on his bookshelf. Most of his books are "how to" books for college entrance examinations. On Sundays, the boy works on examination drills provided by correspondence schools.[13]

Since attending a good university is crucial, many students who fail the examinations the first time choose to wait a year and try again. These students are known as *ronin*, the word used for the lordless samurai in the Tokugawa period. Many applicants spend years trying to get into the university of their choice. Azumi reports that in 1958 there were more than 12,000 applicants for the 2,100 openings at the University of Tokyo. Of the 12,000 applicants, 63 percent were ronin. Of the 2,105 successful applicants, only 26 percent entered straight from high schools, 42 percent had spent one year as ronin, and the remaining 32 percent had spent two or more years as ronin.[14]

The Recruitment Practices

Recruitment of workers in Japan is done in much the same way as in the West, with the exception of recruitment of regular workers of large corporations.[15] Government offices require competitive examinations in Japan as elsewhere. A great majority of those who do not attend universities and those who drop out of the examination rat race seek employment in smaller businesses and minor municipalities. Most of the new employees in these areas enter their employment through personal contacts, advertisements. or public employment offices. In 1964, these three channels accounted for 67 percent of new job placements.[16]

The unique aspect of Japanese recruitment lies in large corporations' hiring of their regular workers.[c] Recruitment is more than merely finding

---

[c]For categories of worker status, see Chapter 7.

qualified workers who are willing to get into a contractual relationship with the firm. Rather, it is more like a family's adoption of children. New recruits are adopted by the corporate family as its "children" who would grow with the company as its "family" members. Companies, for this reason, prefer recruiting only new graduates. Virgin labor is easier to be molded into the company's ways than midcareer recruits. Besides, rank–age correlation can be maintained only by hiring new graduates and placing them at the bottom of the company hierarchy.

As schools and universities are ranked according to their prestige, so are corporations. The best corporations accept applications only from the best schools and universities. (Graduates can apply for a position only through their schools.) Upon receipt of a request from the prospective employer for a list of applicants, the placement office of the school or university selects students to be recommended by carefully weighing the reputation of the firm and the calibre of students. The company screens recommended candidates by means of competitive examinations followed by personal interviews. This procedure is used for all categories of regular workers—managerial, clerical, and blue collar.

The reputation of the candidates' schools and the results of entrance examinations and interviews are still not sufficient to establish the eligibility of prospective candidates for membership in the company. The final step in the selection process of *permanent* workers involves investigations into the family background and personal circumstances of the tentatively accepted candidates. (For nonpermanent regular workers, entrance examinations and personal interviews may suffice.) These investigations are conducted either by the firms's personnel department or by private agencies. Investigations may include a visit to the applicant's home, and discreet inquiries of teachers and neighbors. From these inquiries, the firm may wish to know the following: the health of all the members of the family, particularly the existence or absence of any hereditary diseases of mental instability; the nature of family relationships; the parents' character; the parents' attitude toward the company; the father's social reputation; religious affiliation and behavior of the applicant and the parents; the applicant's and the parents' political views; and the social activities of the applicant involving members of the opposite sex.[17] This concern with the applicant's family background that is not germane to his ability to do the assigned task is highly indicative of Japanese corporations' particularistic relationship with their employees.

Summary

The Japanese education and examination system "locks in" each Japanese youth for life with a predetermined career track. How far or how fast he advances afterwards on the track becomes the function of his age and ability, but he cannot change his track later in life unless it is a downward move. Examinations eliminate successively larger numbers of the youth population at each stage, producing "a pyramid of disappointed people at the base and talented (as defined by the exam) people at the top."[18]

It is a safe estimate that approximately 10 percent of Japan's population belong to the mainstream, elitist occupations; that is, they are affiliated with national government bureaucracies or major corporations. Just as the samurai class ruled the Tokugawa society, contemporary Japan is ruled by the new samurai class—the graduates of the elite universities. Thanks to the familial nature of Japanese social organization, the "new commoners" are not keenly alienated from Japanese society. It is undeniable, however, that there exist mild but ubiquitous feelings of resentment and futility among Japan's second-class citizens. They become obsessed with the idea of placing their children in elite universities, thereby perpetuating the pathological "examination hell."

Notes

1. Ronald Dore, *British Factory, Japanese Factory: The Origins of National Diversity in Industrial Relations* (Berkeley and Los Angeles: University of California Press, 1973), p. 271.

2. For excellent discussions of the Japanese educational system, see: Herbert Passin, *Society and Education in Japan* (New York: Teachers College Press, 1965); and Nathan Glazer, "Social and Cultural Factors in Economic Growth," in Hugh Patrick and Henry Rosovsky, eds., *Asia's New Giant: How the Japanese Economy Works* (Washington, D.C.: The Brookings Institution, 1976), chap. 12.

3. *Japan Almanac 1975* (Tokyo: The Mainichi Newspapers, 1975), p. 226.

4. *Asahi Shinbun*, 19 November 1975.

5. *Japan Economic Journal*, 30 March 1976.

6. *Japan Almanac 1975*, p. 227.

7. Chitoshi Yanaga, *Big Business in Japanese Politics* (New Haven, Conn.: Yale University Press, 1968), p. 24.

8. Akira Kubota, *Higher Civil Servants in Postwar Japan: Their Origins, Educational Background, and Career Patterns* (Princeton, N.J.: Princeton University Press, 1969), pp. 22, 69–70.

9. Ibid., p. 71.

10. For an excellent description of the "examination hell," see: Ezra

Vogel, *Japan's New Middle Class: The Salary Man and His Family in a Tokyo Suburb* (Berkeley and Los Angeles: University of California Press, 1963), chap. III.

11. Yotaro Konaka, "Nada Koko no Todai Ki-Ippon," *Chuo Koron*, April 1975, pp. 216–223.

12. Ibid.

13. Ibid.

14. Koya Azumi, *Higher Education and Business Recruitment in Japan* (New York: Teachers College Press, 1969), p. 27.

15. For excellent discussions of the recruitment practices of Japanese corporations, see: Dore, *British Factory*, chap. 2; and Thomas P. Rohlen, *For Harmony and Strength: Japanese White-Collar Organization in Anthropological Perspective* (Berkeley and Los Angeles: University of California Press, 1974), chap. 3.

16. Robert E. Cole, *Japanese Blue Collar: The Changing Tradition* (Berkeley and Los Angeles: University of California Press, 1971), p. 190.

17. Rohlen, *For Harmony and Strength,* pp. 71–72.

18. Dan Fenno Henderson, *Foreign Enterprise in Japan: Law and Policies* (Chapel Hill, N.C.: University of North Carolina Press, 1973), p. 209.

4   The Government Bureaucracy

Japan has long been a centralized country where the state predominates over individuals and communities. In this chapter we first describe the overall structure of Japanese society, focusing attention on the role played by the state bureaucracy. We then examine the characteristics of the government bureaucracy. Subsequently, the structure of the central government administration and the organization and functions of the economic ministries are studied. In the final section, the relationship between the central and local governments are examined.

The House of Japan

The Japanese statism has its roots in familism. In the traditional Japanese view, the whole nation is a family; what the house is to a biological family, the state is to the national family. The state is not merely a part of the system, but the very framework of it. The Japanese feel that in the beginning there was the nation house called Japan and the people were born into it. Just as the members of the Tokugawa merchant house were subordinate to the authority of the house, so must be the members of the nation to the authority of the state. Although the postwar constitution declares that sovereignty resides with the people, most Japanese neither fully understand its significance nor care about it. The state bureaucrats (*kanryo*) exercise authority not in the name of the people but in the name of the House of Japan. To the Japanese way of thinking, then, the state does not "interfere" with the affairs of private business. It merely manages itself, exercising authority and control over its constituencies. The productive activities of "private business" is very much a part of the business of the whole nation-state.

In premodern Japan, the emperor was the head of the House. He was assisted by the imperial bureaucracy (*kan*) in ruling the people (*min*). Figure 4–1 depicts the structure of contemporary Japanese society. Several differences from the premodern structure may be noted. First, the emperor is no longer the head of the House of Japan; rather, he is a "symbol of national unity." Second, we may note that government has become two-headed. National government bureaucracy (*kanryo*) manages the affairs of the House while the parliamentary government (*seifu*) makes policy decisions. In theory, at least, the government bureaucracy

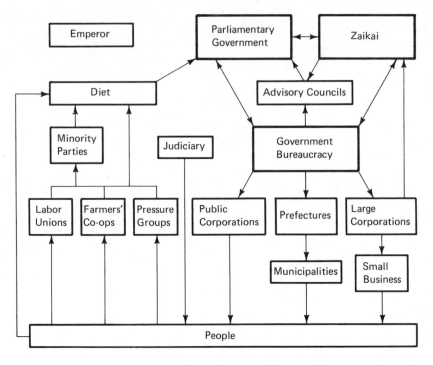

Note: The direction of the arrows indicates the direction of influence.

Figure 4–1. Organization of the House of Japan

is subordinate to the cabinet. In practice, the bureaucracy has power equal to or greater than that of the cabinet. This power derives from the tradition of statism—the prestige and authority associated with the imperial service—and the bureaucrats' superior technology of managing the modern, complex society. The third development in modern Japan is the emergence of the third power center, the *zaikai* (big business leadership). The power of big business derives from its control over money and modern productive technology.

The relationship between the three power centers (kanryo, seifu, and zaikai) is often likened to the traditional game of paper–rock–scissors (*jankenpon*). Paper covers the rock, the rock breaks the scissors, but the scissors in turn cut the paper. Similarly, in the Japanese establishment, no one group is supreme. Ministerial bureaucracy is headed by the politically appointed minister. The key members of the ruling party therefore can influence personnel decisions within the ministry. Moreover, politically ambitious bureaucrats are sensitive to the wishes of influential politicians. The politicians, in turn, must depend heavily on the technical expertise of the bureaucrats in formulating and implementing national policies. The bureaucrats have virtual monopoly in the requisite legal, statistical, and institutional knowledge and administrative technology. Furthermore, as will be discussed later in this chapter, bureaucrats exercise influence in the Diet through their former colleagues who remain loyal and partial to their old ministries.

Bureaucrats have power over the business community by virtue of their project-approving, licensing, and credit-granting authorities. On the other hand, higher officials in the government are sensitive to the wishes of business leaders, since the former must count on the goodwill of the latter in securing attractive positions in business upon retirement from the service. Government officials also need the cooperation of private industry in implementing national policies inasmuch as business corporations have monopoly of productive technology. Turning now to the politician–businessmen relation, we find that politicians can intercede for private firms with ministerial officials in order to obtain a favorable official ruling or quicker approval of an application. Politicians, in turn, must rely heavily on corporations and business organizations for political contributions.

What emerges out of this intricate network of power, influence, and dependency is a jankenpon-like symbiotic relationship. It is further complicated by the elaborate network of interpersonal relations based on school ties, marriage bonds, and ministerial affiliations. Particularly noteworthy is the fact that most of the men who dominate the three power centers are graduates of the elite universities (primarily Tokyo), as well as the fact that government bureaucracy feeds a large number of retired officials into the political arena and the business community. These relations contribute to the club-like atmosphere of the Japanese establishment.

One central feature of Japenese social organization is the curious admixture of the oligarchy (oligopoly) and the streamlined pyramid of authority and control. At the center, a predominant power does not develop; there is a "web of influences and pressures" interweaving through several more or less equally powerful subcenters. Lockwood calls this a "web with no spider."[1] Extending downward from each subcenter is a pyramid of authority and control, often with a considerable amount of two-way (up and down) flows of information and influence. This typical pattern of organization is observed in Figure 4–1, and similar patterns are observable in many subsystems of the House of Japan. For example, in Japan's industrial organization, each industry is dominated by several large firms representing different *keiretsu* groups (see Chapter 8). Each of these firms controls a pyramid of medium- and small-sized firms forming its own enterprise grouping. The Japanese who are conditioned to organize their social structure on a vertical principle seem also to instinctively avoid forming a dominant core of public or private power at the apex of the pyramid.

The Characteristics of the Bureaucracy

The Elite Bureaucrats

The ministerial organization consists of three layers of officials. At the lowest level are the junior staff, doing mostly clerical work. Most of them are high school graduates entering the service upon passing the examinations for junior national government posts. The middle level of bureaucracy is occupied by university graduates who have passed the class B (*otsu*) examinations for senior national government posts. Only those who have passed the class A (*ko*) examinations for senior national government posts are eligible for promotion to the grade of senior staff and above. The class A officials, totaling about ten thousand, constitute the elite core of the national government bureaucracy, towering over the two million national public employees.[2]

In 1976, 1,207 university graduates passed the class A examinations.[3] Each ministry takes somewhere between ten and thirty successful class A candidates per year. The universities they graduated from, and the results of the examinations and interviews, are the major criteria for the ministry's selection of individual applicants. Traditionally, the Ministry of Finance and the Ministry of International Trade and Industry (MITI) vie for the top-ranking candidates. In the ministries, the class A officials are known variously as *kyaria* (career), *erito* (elite), *tokken* (privileged), or *yushikakusha* (qualified). We shall refer to the class A careerists as *career administrators* or *elite bureaucrats*. Class B officials will be called *non-career officials*.

The highest post in the ministerial bureaucracy is the administrative vice-minister. The parliamentary vice-minister is a political appointee, and his role is limited to liaison work between the minister and the Diet. Below the administrative vice-minister are director generals of agencies, bureau chiefs, and the chief of the minister's secretariat, who is equal in rank to a bureau chief. The ministry proper (*honsho*) consists of the minister's secretariat and several bureaus. *Agencies* are quasiautonomous organizations attached to the ministry. Bureaus and agencies are divided into sections which are headed by section chiefs. Some bureaus and agencies have divisions, which are in turn divided into sections. A section may typically have a staff of somewhere between ten and sixty persons. A large section is divided into subsections which are headed by subsection chiefs. Section chiefs are often assisted by assistant section chiefs. The staff below the subsection chief is divided into three grades: senior staff, staff, and junior staff.

While noncareer officials remain in given positions for many years, career administrators are transferred from position to position within the ministry, and are sometimes assigned to other ministries, prefectural governments, or overseas positions. Personnel reshufflings of career bureaucrats take place every one and one-half to two years. In about thirty years after entering the service, about one in six careerists reaches the bureau chief level. For the vice-ministership, the ratio is one in thirty.[4]

Hierarchical Order

Within a ministry, bureaus and agencies are ranked according to their prestige and power. In the Ministry of International Trade and Industry (MITI), for example, the chief of the Industrial Policy Bureau is the highest ranking official under the vice-minister. Then come the director generals of the three affiliated agencies, followed by the chief of the International Trade Policy Bureau, the Machinery and Information Industries Bureau, and so on.[5]

In the ministerial bureaucracy, all the elite bureaucrats who enter the ministry in any given year climb the ladder with the same speed. There is an unwritten rule that those who enter the ministry in a given year cannot serve under those who entered in the same year or later. Thus, when one of the bureau chiefs is promoted to vice-minister, the other bureau chiefs who have the same length of service as the new vice-minister resign. Although those in the same year-of-entry class advance at the same speed, the position to which an official is assigned reveals a lot about his chances of reaching the top. For example, in the Finance Ministry, the chief of the Budget Bureau customarily becomes the vice-minister. In the MITI, the chief of the Industrial Policy Bureau is normally the top contender for the vice-ministership. Similarly, all the way down to the most recent class of entry, the brightest and most promising men in each class occupy the most prestigious positions at each level. Those who move from a key position to another are said to be on the "elite course." Whether or not an official actually reaches the top depends largely on his personality, competence, alma mater (the non-Tokyo graduate has one strike against him), clique membership (belonging to the vice-minister's clique is a big plus), and the personal likes and dislikes of the minister. The preferences of the majority party leaders and the key zaikai leaders may also influence the selection process, especially near the top.

The Tokyo University Bias

We observed in the preceding chapter that the graduates of the University of Tokyo (Tokyo Daigaku, or Todai for short) wield conspicuous influence in Japanese society. The concentration of Todai graduates is particularly pronounced at the higher echelons of the national government bureaucracy. For example, in 1974, eleven out of the twelve highest ranking officials of the MITI were Tokyo graduates. The predominance of Todai graduates in government bureaucracy can be accounted for as follows: having been established in 1886 as the Imperial University with a specific purpose of training government officials, it was for many years the only university in Japan. Its graduates enjoyed the privilege of entering the newly established national government service without entrance examinations. It thus attracted the brightest young men from all over the nation. The university and the graduates developed a strong sense of leadership and elitism. As the number of universities later proliferated, the Imperial University graduates solidified their school ties by developing a Todai clique in the government bureaucracy.

Ingroup favoritism of Todai graduates is very subtle and difficult to prove. By its very nature, Todai attracts the brightest young minds of Japan. Its graduates far outnumber graduates of any other university in passing the class A examinations for senior government posts. Consequently, there are a disproportionately large number of Todai graduates in the national government bureaucracy, and the highest levels of bureaucratic hierarchies are almost completely dominated by them. Under these circumstances, favoritism is "not only probable but also less provable."[6]

Descent from Heaven

We have earlier observed that bureau chiefs retire in their early fifties to avoid working under the newly promoted vice-minister who entered the ministry in the same year as they did. The new vice-minister himself customarily retires within two or three years. (Between 1949 and 1974, the MITI had fourteen administrative vice-ministers.) Retiring senior bureaucrats seldom fail to find attractive second careers. In fact, the whole system is predicated upon the presumption that elite bureaucrats have two careers. The first career in the bureaucracy is regarded as a stepping stone to a more financially rewarding second career in private or public corporations.

The practice of higher administrators securing postcareer employment in business and public corporations is commonly known as *amakudari* (parachuting; literally, "descent from heaven"). Years before their anticipated retirement, bureaucrats begin cultivating the goodwill of influential politicians and important business executives by doing them many favors. The higher their positions are and hence the closer their retirement is, the more sensitive they are to the wishes of private industry and political parties. Herein lies one important factor contributing to the symbiotic relationship between bureaucrats, politicians, and businessmen.

Most ministries have under their wing a host of public corporations and semipublic institutions to which they can send their retiring officials. (Important appointments must be approved by the cabinet.) Naturally, the larger and more powerful ministries have a larger number of such outlets. Those few ministries which do not have public corporations under their jurisdiction find their own unique solutions. Thus, retiring officials of the Foreign Ministry become ambassadors. The Local Autonomy Ministry officials descend to local governments. The Economic Planning Agency has established a few research institutes for some of its former bureau chiefs. Between 1955 and 1972, 322 bureau chiefs and vice-ministers retired from the five largest ministries (Finance, MITI, Transportation, Agriculture, and Construction). Practically all of them had second careers: nearly three-quarters of the jobs were found in private and public corporations. The breakdown is shown below.[7]

The Diet	27
Public corporations	108
Private corporations	122
Business organizations	34
Government agencies[a]	6
Teaching, law	10
Others[b]	15

For the retiring senior bureaucrats of the "economic" ministries, second careers in private corporations are attractive alternatives. Most of the officials who go to private corporations are from the three ministries—Finance, MITI, and Transportation. The Finance Ministry officials traditionally go to banks, the MITI bureaucrats become officers of manufacturing and utilities companies, and the Transportation officials descend to airlines and shipping companies. In other words, bureaucrats entering business go to companies that have close working relations with their ministry. Corporations employ these bureaucrats notwithstanding their innate reluctance to accept outsiders for several reasons: First, these

[a]Include the Bank of Japan.

[b]Include unemployed.

officials are extremely capable men of proven track record. Second, the firms may owe the officials some debts (*kari*) which must be repaid. Third, these former bureaucrats are intimately familiar with all the elements of project approving and licensing procedures in the ministry. Fourth, they know influential officials in the ministry as their former colleagues, subordinates, kohai, or kobun. Such personal connections are naturally very valuable to the business firms.

Temporary External Assignment

Career administrators are frequently transferred from bureau to bureau within the same ministry. In this process, they acquire broad knowledge and understanding of the diverse functions of the ministry. They are seldom transferred, however, to a position outside the ministry. A government official is "reborn" into a ministerial family as a MITI man or a Finance man, and remains there until he retires.

Permanent transfers are rare, but transfers to an outside position on a temporary basis are quite common. This practice is known as *shukko* (temporary external assignment). A career official is assigned to an external position, not as a mere liaison officer, but as a regular staff member of the new organization. For example, a young Finance man may be assigned to head a provincial tax office for a few years. Or, a young MITI bureaucrat, not old enough to be a section chief in the ministry, may be dispatched to a prefectural government to serve as a section chief there. While these officials are on external assignment, they keep their seniority in, and identity with, their ministry. From the receiving agency's point of view, they are regular employees, except that they are men of guaranteed intellectual capacity and are also useful in serving as a valuable link with the central ministries. Upon returning to *honsho* (the ministry proper), the young careerist is invariably promoted to a higher position. After serving in the ministry for a few years, he may be transferred out again. Each time he moves up in rank. He settles down in the ministry, however, by the time he becomes a bureau chief. If he realizes that his chances of becoming a bureau chief are poor, he tries to settle down permanently in one of his shukko positions (or else actively seeks an amakudari position to retire to).

Some of the national government agencies to which the MITI sends its careerists on temporary tours of duty are: Ministry of Foreign Affairs, Economic Planning Agency, Defense Agency, Science and Technology Agency, Fair Trade Commission, Cabinet Secretariat, Prime Minister's Office, and Hokkaido Development Agency.[8] It also sends its young officials to its eight regional bureaus, as well as to important prefectures, to serve as section and division chiefs primarily in the areas of commercial and industrial affairs.

The system of shukko does not ordinarily affect the power relations among ministries, since the number of outsiders in a given ministry is relatively very small. There is, however, an important exception to this rule. When a new agency or ministry is established, the career staff members must initially come from outside. The problem with this arrangement is that those who come from outside do not consider themselves as the members of the new organization, but remain loyal and partial to their "home" ministry or agency. Only those officials who are recruited by the new agency straight from universities consider themselves genuine members of the new organization. Until the homegrown careermen rise through the ranks, the key positions in the new agency are monopolized by the shukko "colonists" and the agency is subjected to external controls exerted through them. For over twenty years since its inception in 1946, the Economic Planning Agency (EPA) had been controlled by the shukko officials from the MITI and the Finance Ministry. The agency began recruiting its own careerists in 1956. As late as 1974, 110 of the agency's 210 elite bureaucrats were shukko officials from other ministries.[9] The homegrown EPA careerists began exercising control over the agency in December 1969 when, for the first time, one of them was appointed deputy director general (vice-minister).

Bureaucrats-Turned-Politicians

The power and influence of bureaucrats as a group are enhanced by the recent tendency of a large number of retired bureaucrats entering politics. Article 68 of the constitution stipulates that the majority of cabinet members must hold seats in the Diet. By custom, virtually all the cabinet members are now selected from the Diet. The implication of this practice is that politically ambitious bureaucrats must run for election to a Diet seat after they retire from office. Thanks to the immense prestige associated with high government positions, many former bureaucrats have found it relatively easy to get elected to the Diet. It is estimated that about one-third of the parliament members have been bureaucrats.[10] The Ministry of Finance has a larger number of former officials in the Diet than any other government agency. In 1974, nineteen members of the House of Representatives and eight members of the House of Councilors were former Finance bureaucrats. Two of the lower-house members—T. Fukuda (former chief of the Budget Bureau) and M. Ohira (formerly Minister's Secretary)—were then top contenders for the premiership.[11]

Just as amakudari contributes to the symbiotic relationship between government bureaucracy and the business community, the practice of retired senior officials entering politics contributes to a close working relationship between politicians and bureaucrats. Ambitious bureaucrats, preparing themselves for a political career, become highly sensitive to pressures from political parties. Furthermore, bureaucrats-turned-politicians form a formidable power block in coalition with bureaucrats in active service. In standing committees of the Diet, former government officials behave in ways partial to the ministry in which they once served. This bureaucratic brotherhood in national politics is often referred to as *kanbatsu* (bureaucratic clique).

Bureaucrats as Lawmakers

The concept of the separation of power into executive, legislative, and judicial is a relatively recent import from the West. The traditional Japanese *kanri* (imperial official) was a lawmaker, administrator, and judge rolled into one. This tradition, coupled with the complexity of managing a modern nation state, gives the present-day Japanese bureaucrats an inordinate amount of legislative power. In fact, more than 90 percent of the laws enacted are prepared and submitted to the Diet by various ministries.[12] Furthermore, bureaucrats draft reports of various advisory councils, as we shall see in the next chapter. The Japanese bureaucrats thus practically make the very law they administer. Such laws would naturally reflect the values and wishes of bureaucrats, and give them maximum authority and discretionary power.

Administrative Guidance

Administrative guidance (*gyosei shido*) is a unique Japanese practice, according to which government officials or agencies guide industries and firms in desired directions by informal means and without specific statutory authorities. The ministries and agencies justify the use of this device by invoking the broad statutory mandate of the laws establishing them, which invariably state that they are responsible for promoting, regulating, and guiding the development of industries under their jurisdiction. The Japanese academic thinking leans toward the view that specific statutory authority is not required for administrative guidance.[13] Under the authority of this blanket mandate, the ministerial officials summon representatives of a firm or an industry to their offices and express (often strongly) their wishes or expectations couched in such terms as requests, recommendations, and suggestions. Compliance is voluntary, but the officials do not hesitate to use various carrots and sticks, which are often totally unrelated to the issue at hand.[c]

The practice of administrative guidance is part and parcel of Japan's government–business symbiosis. Businessmen and industrialists are fully aware that ministerial officials have in their minds the best interests of the industries and the national economy. Thus, when the officials "'recommend" or "suggest" that the firms increase or decrease production, limit or fix prices, build or not build a plant, or merge with another company, little overt hostility or resentment is generated. Firms or industry become recalcitrant only when they feel that they are treated unequally, or when they sense that the government's proposed measure would threaten their survival. Under normal circumstances, administrative guidance is regarded as the price businesses have to pay for the services rendered by the government in providing protection, orderly market, and the long and broad view of the economy.

We must also remember that the government–business relation is a two-way street. At the very high level of administrative bureaucracy, there exists keen sensitivity to the wishes of the business community. The practice of amakudari, the political ambitions of higher bureaucrats, and contributions of political funds by corporations and business organizations, combine to make industry's influence over the government just as strong as the bureaucratic power over the industry.

The Economic Ministries

In 1974, there were twelve ministers heading an equal number of ministries, and eight state ministers without portfolio heading various agencies.[d] Of the various ministries and agencies, the following three—the Ministry of Finance, the MITI, and the EPA—are of particular interest to us because of the important roles they play in the nation's economic affairs. We now turn to examinations of the organizational structure and functions of these ministries.

---

[c]See Chapter 8 for the MITI's promotion of "guidance cartels"; see Chapter 9 for the Bank of Japan and its "window guidance."

[d]The twelve ministries are: Justice, Foreign Affairs, Finance, Education, Health and Welfare, Agriculture and Forestry, International Trade and Industry, Transportation, Posts and Telecommunications, Labor, Construction, and Local Autonomy. Additionally, thirteen agencies and commissions are attached to the Prime Minister's Office. The more important ones are: Fair Trade Commission, Imperial Household Agency, Administrative Management Agency, Defense Agency, Economic Planning Agency, Environment Agency, and National Land Agency.

The Ministry of Finance[14]

The Ministry of Finance (MOF, *Okura-sho*) is responsible for the nation's monetary and fiscal policies. Monetary policy is concerned with regulating the availability and cost of credit, while fiscal policy deals with government expenditures, taxes, and debt. Through these policies, the government can regulate the allocation of resources in the national economy, affect the distribution of income and wealth among its citizens, stabilize the level of economic activities, and generally promote economic growth and welfare. In achieving these objectives, various types of policy instruments are used, which include: supervision of the Bank of Japan in carrying out its monetary policy, formation of annual budget and control of government expenditure programs, allocation of public investment and loan funds, formation of tax policies and collection of taxes, formulation and execution of social insurance and pension programs, management of national properties, and control of foreign exchanges and formulation of exchange-rate policies. These controls represent the most basic aspects of the management of the nation's economy. Through controls over the nation's purse strings, the MOF exerts a vast and omnipresent influence over the direction of the Japanese economy.[e]

The Minister's Secretariat and the seven bureaus (Budget, Tax, Customs and Tariff, Financial, Securities, Banking, and International Finance) comprise the *honsho* (the ministry proper). The honsho staff numbers about 2,000 persons, most of whom are elite bureaucrats. The three ancillary bureaus (Mint, Printing, and Customs) perform mundane administrative and technical functions, but they do not participate in policy making. The ten regional finance bureaus are known as mini-MOFs. They serve as pipelines between the honsho and regional economies by feeding local information to the ministry and supervising the implementation of MOF policies in each region. Affiliated with the ministry as a semiautonomous *gaikyoku* (external agency) is the National Tax Administration Agency. With a total staff of over 52,000 persons, the agency administers collection of national taxes through its 498 tax offices located throughout the country.

We now turn to brief examinations of the organization and functions of the Finance Ministry's more important honsho bureaus.

The Budget Bureau. This bureau is the most powerful and prestigious of all the bureaus in the ministry because of its control over formulation, execution, and accounting of the national budget. The twelve budget officers are the front-line officials of the bureau and the ministry. They

---

[e]Monetary and fiscal policies will be discussed in Chapters 9 and 10.

examine the budget requests submitted by various ministries and agencies, appraise them, negotiate with appropriate officials in each ministry and agency, meet lobbyists from local governments and special interest groups, and draw up a preliminary budget which will be presented to the Diet for approval.[f]

The Tax Bureau. This is a relatively small bureau. In addition to the General Affairs Section, the bureau has four other sections dealing with four different types of tax. The primary responsibility of the bureau is the formulation of national taxation policies and procedures. It drafts new tax laws and proposes revisions of the existing tax laws. In other words, while the Budget Bureau determines how to spend the money, the Tax Bureau devises the ways to raise the money.

The activities of this bureau reach a peak in the fall of every year. Draft tax reform proposals must be presented to the Tax System Study Council (*Zeisei Chosa-kai*), which, in turn, must report its findings to the prime minister by the end of the year. Although the recommendations are made in the name of the council, actual work is done by the Tax Bureau officials. The ideas on tax reforms and new taxes may originate anywhere: they may come from the prime minister, the minority parties, the council, or from within the bureau. The bureau staff then collects and studies relevant data, gives the idea a general shape, and formulates a tentative revision proposal. In doing so, it must speculate on the possible reactions of the cabinet, minority parties, business leadership, and the mass media. Thus, virtually every day and night in early fall, the key officials of the bureau gather in the bureau chief's office and engage in endless, heated discussions. After the council has started its deliberations, the high ranking officials of the bureau actively engage in *nemawashi* (spadework or buttonholing) with members of the Diet in an effort to obtain their backing of the upcoming tax-reform bill.

The Financial Bureau. Outside the Minister's Secretariat, the Financial Bureau is the largest bureau in the ministry with thirteen sections. The bureau is responsible for the management of government bonds, handling of the treasury business (administration of revenues and expenditures, issuance of coins, etc.), management of national properties, management of the Trust Fund Special Account, and the development and management of the Fiscal Investment and Loan Program (FILP).[g]

The bureau is also responsible for administering receipts and disbursements of funds through the government accounts set up with the

---

[f]The types of budget will be discussed in Chapter 10.

[g]The Trust Fund Special Account and the FILP will be discussed in Chapter 10.

Bank of Japan. Receipts and disbursements must be balanced carefully in order to avoid causing unnecessary fluctuations in the size of the nation's money supply. Issuance and retirement of government bonds and notes must be finely adjusted for the same reason. The bureau also regulates the total supply of money in the economy. Although issuance of currency is the responsibility of the Bank of Japan, the size of the total money supply (coins, currency, and commercial bank demand deposits) is determined by the Financial Bureau.

The Banking Bureau. This bureau is responsible for the formuation of the nation's monetary policy as well as regulation and supervision of all the financial institutions, including the Bank of Japan. The ministry of Finance's Banking Bureau is legally empowered to supervise the Bank of Japan, which must receive approvals from the ministry for issuing, altering or abolishing some of its key rules and regulations. The ministry (technically the cabinet) also appoints some key officers of the Bank.

Under the current laws the Ministry of Finance is empowered to regulate and supervise the organization, management, and accounting of financial institutions ranging from commercial banks to insurance companies. To establish a banking business, for instance, requires a license from the ministry. The ministry's approval is also necessary for changing the size of capital stock, establishing a branch office, and merging with another bank. The ministry can also request reports from the bank management on its operations, inspect bank assets and operations, order dismissal of bank officers or suspension of the banks' business, and revoke the license to operate banking business. Thus, the power and authority of the Ministry of Finance and its Banking Bureau over the banking community is overwhelming.[h]

The Ministry of International Trade and Industry[15]

While the Finance Ministry controls the monetary and financial aspects of the economy, the Ministry of International Trade and Industry (MITI; *Tsusho Sangyo-sho*, or *Tsusan-sho* for short) is responsible for the regulation of the production and distribution of goods and services. As the steward of Japanese industry, the MITI provides business with order and a sense of direction. It also does a great deal of planning concerning the structure of Japanese industry.

Specifically, the MITI has six broad functions. First, it is responsible for the control of Japan's foreign trade. Promotion of trade, management

[h]See Chapter 9 for the Bank of Japan and its monetary policy.

of foreign exchanges related to trade flows, and international cooperation on trade matters are MITI's responsibilities. The ministry must make sure that Japanese industries are supplied with adequate amounts of imported resources. It must also promote an orderly expansion of Japanese exports. Second, the MITI is responsible for assuring the smooth flow of goods in the national economy. It is a MITI's task to promote, improve, and adjust the production, distribution, and consumption of mining and manufacturing products. It is the responsibilities of the ministry to assure adequate supplies of goods at reasonable prices, and regulate and inspect production of goods for which it has set safety standards. Third, the MITI has jurisdiction over the manufacturing, mining, and distribution industries, and is charged with the task of promoting their development and adjusting, regulating, and guiding their activities. The MITI draws authority for its industrial policy from this requirement. (The MITI's industrial policy will be discussed in Chapter 8.) Fourth, the ministry is charged with the responsibility for securing a stable supply of industrial raw materials and energy resources for the national economy. As part of its resource and energy policy, the ministry works to develop new overseas sources of materials and fuels, promotes the development of nuclear energy, and regulates electric and natural gas companies. These tasks are administered by the Resource and Energy Agency. Fifth, the MITI administers the government's small business policy. Through its Small and Medium Enterprises Agency, it promotes and guides the development of small businesses. Last, through its Patent Office, the ministry handles the administration of patents and trade marks.

Of these six functions, the first three are the MITI's primary functions. It controls international trade, regulates production and distribution of goods, and shapes the structure of Japanese industry. Administrative guidance, buttressed by the ministry's licensing and project approving authorities, is used as the main instrument for carrying out these tasks.

The MITI honsho has seven bureaus and the Minister's Secretariat, with a total staff of about 2,300 persons. Affiliated with the ministry are the three semiautonomous agencies, serving the last three of the six functions enumerated above. Eight regional MITI bureaus provide feedback from local economies. One of the unique features of the MITI organization is the distinction between the five general (or ''horizontal'') bureaus and the three specific (or ''vertical'') industrial bureaus. The Minister's Secretariat and the other four general bureaus (International Trade Policy, International Trade Administration, Industrial Policy, and Industrial Location and Environmental Protection) provide a broad policy direction, while the three vertical industrial bureaus (Basic Industries, Machinery and Information Industries, and Consumer Goods Industries) implement government policies in each industry under the bureau's jurisdiction. The power and influence of the MITI are exercised primarily through the close working relations between its industrial bureaus and the industries and firms under their supervision. The functions of the more important bureaus are briefly discussed below.

The International Trade Administration Bureau. Promotion and adjustment of exports and imports, control of foreign exchanges related to trade, export inspection, and export insurance are the main responsibilities of this bureau.

Japan's foreign trade is controlled under the Foreign Exchange and Trade Control Law, Export Trade Law, Import Trade Law, and the MITI ordinances and rules pertaining to these laws. These rules are complicated and changed frequently. Different types of goods in different quantities are subject to licensing or approval by different agencies. The bureau is the ultimate authority on the applicability of these rules; it issues detailed interpretations and explanations of the relevant laws, ordinances, and rules.

The Industrial Policy Bureau. This bureau is the brain of the MITI. Its responsibility is broadscope policy making for the entire economy. As such, it is the most important bureau in the ministry, and the bureau's chief is the highest ranking official in the ministry under the vice-minister.

Industrial policy is government policy designed to reshape the structure of the productive capacity and activity of various industries. By government policy, production and investment are encouraged in some industries and discouraged in others (see Chapters 5 and 8). In formulating this policy, the Industrial Policy Bureau works closely with the Industrial Structure Council (*Sankoshin*) [see Chapter 5]. The bureau's secondary functions are the protection of general consumer interest, control of prices, regulation of foreign investments in Japan, and coordination of activities with the Japan Chamber of Commerce and Industry.

The Industrial Bureaus. There are three bureaus that are known as industrial (or vertical) bureaus. Each of these bureaus supervises a certain number of industries as their *genkyoku* (bureau of primary jurisdiction). The following list of the sections in each bureau indicates the scope of the bureau's responsibilities.

The Basic Industries Bureau. General Affairs, Iron and Steel Administration, Iron and Steel Production, Nonferrous Metal Products, Basic Chemicals, Chemical Products, and Chemical Fertilizers.

The Machinery and Information Industries Bureau. General Affairs, International Trade, Industrial Machinery, Cast and Wrought Products, Electronics Policy, Data Processing Promotion, Electronics and Electric Machinery, Automobiles, Weight and Measures, Aircraft and Ordnances, Bicycles and Motor Cycles, and Machinery Credit Insurance.

The Consumer Goods Bureau. General Affairs, International Trade, Fiber and Spinning, Textile Products, Paper and Pulp, Household and Sundry Goods, Recreational Goods, Ceramics and Construction Materials, and Housing Industry.

The Agency of Natural Resources and Energy. The agency is composed of the Director General's Secretariat, the Petroleum Department, the Coal Department, and the Public Utilities Department. The agency's responsibilities include the formation of long-range resource and energy policies, assurance of stable supplies of energy resources for the national economy, promotion of efficient uses of fuels, and solution of the pollution problems related to energy resources.

Although the agency is technically a semiautonomous, external bureau of the MITI, for all practical purposes it functions as just another honsho bureau. As such, it serves as *genkyoku* (bureau of primary jurisdiction) to the petroleum refining, petroleum products, nonferrous metal mining, coal mining, coal products, electricity and natural gas, and atomic energy industries.

The Small and Medium Enterprises Agency. This agency consists of the Director General's Secretariat, the Planning Department, and the Guidance Department. The agency's responsibility is to foster the development of smaller enterprises. It gathers and analyzes information concerning economic problems of smaller enterprises, mediates credit for them, solicits cooperation of other government agencies on matters related to smaller enterprises, and promotes the development of technology and management techniques helpful to smaller firms.

The Economic Planning Agency

The Economic Planning Agency (EPA, *Keizai Kikaku-cho)* is a small agency attached to the Prime Minister's Office. Under the director general of cabinet rank, there are six bureaus, which are: Director General's Secretariat, Coordination Bureau, Economic Welfare Bureau, Price Bureau, Comprehensive Planning Bureau, and Research Bureau. The

Comprehensive Planning Bureau works closely with the Economic Council (*Keizai Shingi-kai*) in formulating long-range economic plans (see Chapter 5).

Central–Local Government Relations

The Japanese constitution declares that local public entities shall have the right to manage their affairs "in accordance with the principle of local autonomy" (Article 92). In practice, local autonomy is highly circumscribed by the centralizing tendencies of the national government. Authority, finance, and personnel matters are centralized—so much so that prefectures and muncipalities are virtually departments or branch offices of the national government.[16]

Local Government Finance

In 1974, 48 percent of the national government revenue was returned to local governments in the forms of grants and subsidies. These moneys constituted about 47 percent of the latter's revenues (see Chapter 10). Specific subsidies tend to have detrimental effects on the development of local autonomy. Applications for subsidies must be approved, case by case, by competent ministries and agencies. The national government officials must be convinced that the need for the proposed project exists, approve the estimated amount of the subsidy, approve the proposed project, and inspect the project at various stages. Most projects require approval by more than one ministry or agency. For example, negotiations for a national aid in the construction of a rural road may require approvals of the following ministries: Finance, Transportation, Construction, Agriculture, Local Autonomy, and the National Land Agency. Each ministry and agency naturally wants to control that aspect of the project that falls within its competence.

Officials from every prefecture in Japan are continually pouring into Tokyo to conduct negotiations with various ministries. Steiner cites the case of a prefecture where the governor spends about one week in four in Tokyo, and department heads spend on the average five to seven days every two months there.[17] The inevitable byproduct of the excessive financial dependence of local governments on Tokyo is, of course, the increasing centralization of power in Tokyo. Local government officials have become extremely responsive to the wishes of the central government bureaucracy. Thus, a mere notification by a ministry to governors or division chiefs tends to acquire the force of law. It is obeyed whether or not it is legally binding.[18]

Centralized Authority

Centralized control is exercised not only through extralegal channels but also by statutory means. It must be remembered that Japan's legal structure is unitary. "Law" means national law; it is equally applicable throughout the country. Local entities do not enact laws. The Local Autonomy Law of 1947—the basic law for the implementation of the provisions of Article 92 of the constitution—spells out in detail the organization and functions of local governments, as well as their rights and responsibilities. Other laws stipulate in detail what local entities can and cannot do. For example, the Local Tax Law specifies what types of tax local governments can and must levy and at what rates. Although the Local Finance Law provides that local governments can issue their own bonds, Article 250 of the Local Autonomy Law stipulates that "for the time being, the Ministry of Local Autonomy shall be empowered to approve applications for local bond issues." The Local Autonomy Ministry gives priorities, in approving bond issues, to projects to which it is giving subsidies. The Finance Ministry each year determines the total volume of local bond issues in conjunction with its overall fiscal policy.

National Functions Assigned to Local Governments

In accordance with the provisions of the Local Autonomy Law Articles 146 and 150, the national government imposes a considerable number of national functions (e.g., the management of rivers, census registry, national elections, etc.) to chief executives of municipalities and prefectures, and to prefectural commissions. This delegation of authority is known as *agency delegation*. In performing these functions the local chief executives or commissions, acting as national government agents, are responsible to the national government, and not to the local assembly.[19] That the local chief executive is subordinate to the national government is explicitly stated by Article 15 of the National Government Organization Law: "with respect to affairs under his charge each minister may direct and supervise the heads of local public entities in respect to national administrative affairs which they execute . . ."[20] Furthermore, Article 146 of the Local Autonomy Law provides that a governor who is derelict of assigned duties may be removed from office by the prime minister.[21]

National and Local Civil Services

The principle of the separation of the national and local civil services exists in name only as far as the employees of the national and prefectural governments are concerned. Especially noteworthy is the common practice of dispatching national government officials to prefectures on a *shukko* (temporary external assignment) basis. Many high ranking positions in prefectural governments are occupied by the officials sent from the central government. In 1974, 23 general affairs division chiefs and an equal number of financial section chiefs in the nation's 47 prefectures were dispatched officials from the Local Autonomy Ministry.[22] They serve as local civil servants, but their seniority and pension rights in their home ministry continue uninterrupted. Local governments benefit from this arrangement because they can use these officials as valuable lines of communication with the central authorities. The ministry does not find this practice objectionable, since its influence in prefectures can be enhanced by it. As we have already noted, alternate assignments of young career officials in and out of the ministry are considered an important aspect of their training. Kusayanagi explains how this system works: About a year after entering the Local Autonomy Ministry, the young careerist is sent to a prefecture for a short while as an apprentice section chief (an unofficial title). After spending two or three years back in the ministry, he is dispatched to another prefecture, this time as a section chief. He returns to a position of assistant section chief at the ministry after two or three years' stay in the country. The next time he leaves the ministry, he will be a section chief in a key prefecture or a division chief in a smaller prefecture.[23]

Conclusion

Historically, Japan has long been a highly centralized country. After World War II, the "principle of local autonomy" became, in theory at least, an integral part of the Japanese political system. Traditional attitudes die hard, however. The reality remains greatly at variance with the law. The relationship between the central government and local governments is still essentially one of superior and subordinate. For all practical purposes, local governments are extensions of the central government bureaucracy.

Notes

1. William W. Lockwood, ed., *The State and Economic Enterprise in Japan: Essays in the Political Economy of Growth* (Princeton, N.J.: Princeton University Press, 1965), p. 503.

2. Joji Watanuki, "Minshu Shugi no Toji Noryoku," *Chuo Koron*, May 1975, p. 85.

3. *Japan Economic Journal*, 30 March 1976.

4. Taro Kawamoto, "Sore demo Todai Hogaku-bu wa Nihon o Ugokasu," *Bungei Shunju*, September 1972, p. 173.

5. Taro Nawa, *Tsusan-sho* [MITI] (Tokyo: Kyoikusha, 1974), p. 126.

6. Akira Kubota, *Higher Civil Servants in Postwar Japan: Their Origins, Educational Background, and Career Patterns* (Princeton, N.J.: Princeton University Press. 1969). p. 89.

7. Nikkei Business Henshu-bu, *Nihon no Kigyo Kankyo* [The environment of Japanese business] (Tokyo: Nihon Keizai Shinbun-sha, 1974), p. 185.

8. Nawa, *Tsusan-sho*, p. 147.

9. Daizo Kusayanagi, "Kuge no Yakata Keizai Kikaku-cho," *Bungei Shunju*, December 1974, p. 123.

10. Takeshi Ishida, *Japanese Society* (New York: Random House, 1971), p. 71, cited in S. Prakash Sethi, *Japanese Business and Social Conflict* (Cambridge, Mass.: Ballinger Publishing Co., 1975), p. 30.

11. Kazuo Yasuhara, *Okura-sho* [Ministry of Finance] (Tokyo: Kyoikusha, 1974), pp. 221–223.

12. Chitoshi Yanaga, *Big Business in Japanese Politics* (New Haven, Conn.: Yale University Press, 1968), p. 105.

13. See Dan Fenno Henderson, *Foreign Enterprise in Japan: Law and Politics* (Chapel Hill, N.C.: University of North Carolina Press, 1973), pp. 204–206.

14. The discussion of this subsection is drawn largely from Yasuhara, *Okura-sho*.

15. The discussion in this subsection is drawn largely from Nawa, *Tsusan-sho*, chapter II.

16. An excellent source of information on Japan's local government is Kurt Steiner, *Local Government in Japan* (Stanford, Calif.: Stanford University Press, 1965).

17. Ibid., p. 321.

18. Ibid., p. 316.

19. Ibid., p. 237.

20. Ibid., p. 315.

21. Ibid., p. 314.

22. Daizo Kusayanagi, ''Kamen Raida Jichi-cho,'' *Bungei Shunju*, January 1975, p. 186.

23. Ibid.

5

Quasi-Government Institutions

The traditional absence in Japan of the consciousness of a clear-cut distinction between the public and the private (in the Western sense) has resulted in the development of a large gray zone between government and business activities. In the areas of transportation, communication, housing, and finance, *public enterprises* make significant contributions. In public policy formation, numerous *advisory councils* provide inputs to the governmental decision-making process. In this chapter we examine these two quasi-government institutions.

Public Enterprises

Definition and Classification

The relative importance of public enterprises in directly productive activities is one of the salient characteristics of the Japanese economy. Of the approximately 4.9 million public employees (1974), about 25 percent are employees of public enterprises. In the national government, some 43 percent of the personnel are employed by public enterprises. Although the national and local public enterprises combined employ only about 2.2 percent of the country's total labor force, their role in the nation's economic, social, and political life is far more significant than the number suggests. This is because of the nature of their activities: they provide such important services as transportation, communication, finance, and public housing. When the employees of public corporations and government enterprises[a] struck in the fall of 1975, the economy was nearly paralyzed.

Although the term "public enterprise" (*ko-kigyo*) is widely used by the mass media, it lacks a clear-cut definition. The term is nowhere found in the statute; therefore, it lacks legal content. Generally, it refers to a bewildering array of enterprises and activities that are associated with public bodies. For our purposes, however, the following definition may

---

[a]The five government enterprises (*go-gengyo*) are: postal service, forest service, printing, mint, and alcohol monopoly. Since these activities are run directly by the government, their employees are classified as public servants.

62

suffice: Public enterprises are "business organizations that are wholly or partially owned by governments and effectively controlled by them but that operate as commercial enterprises."[1] Following this definition, we include in our discussion those mixed enterprises that are established by the government but invite private capital participation.

Table 5–1 lists the various types of public enterprises. Although local public enterprises far outnumber national enterprises, the latter are far more important in terms of their sizes. In what follows our discussion is limited to national public enterprises.

Public enterprises can be classified into two broad categories: public corporations, and special private banks and corporations. Public corporations are created by special laws. They have a corporate personality, but do not assume a joint-stock form. Their capital is either totally or partially subscribed by the government. Special private banks and corporations are similarly created by special laws, but they are essentially private joint-stock companies or cooperatives. Having been established at a government initiative and created by an act of the legislature, they enjoy special privileges but are subject to close governmental supervision.

Public Corporations

Of the ninety-eight public corporations now in existence, only two (the Metropolitan Area Rapid Transit Authority and the Japan Scholarship

Table 5–1
Public Enterprises in Japan

Categories	Number of Enterprises	Number of Personnel
National public enterprises[a]	112	919,743
Public corporations	98	879,453
"Public service" corporations	3	781,438
"Construction & development" corporations	16	33,563
"Project" corporations	20	21,106
"Loan & finance" corporations	10	9,461
Special public banks	2	1,497
Other public corporations	47	32,388
Special private banks	2	9,098
Special private corporations	12	31,192
Local public enterprises[b]	6,926	310,300
Total public enterprises	7,038	1,230,043

Source: Administrative Management Agency, *Tokushu Hojin Soran, showa 50-nen ban* (Tokyo: Ministry of Finance, Printing Bureau, 1975), pp. 307–312; Ministry of Local Autonomy, *Chiho Jichi Hakusho, showa 50-nen ban* (Tokyo: Ministry of Finance, Printing Bureau, 1975), pp. 110–111.

[a]As of January 1, 1975.

[b]Waterworks, hospitals, local transport systems, etc., as of March 31, 1974.

Society) date back from the prewar years. The rapid proliferation of the number of public corporations since the end of the war can be attributed to several factors. First, the Allied occupation authorities encouraged the creation of semiautonomous government enterprises in order to "democratize" the Japanese economy. Consequently, the three "public service" corporations (kosha) were created out of the existing government enterprises.

Second, during periods of reconstruction and rapid growth of the Japanese economy in the 1950s and 1960s, many social and economic needs arose that required governmental action. The traditional ministerial system, however, seemed ill-suited for meeting these needs as compared to the managerial and financial devices of autonomous corporations. The use of public corporations, it was believed, could assure freedom of management while avoiding overburdening the central government administrative machinery. On the other hand, the nature of the economic and social services needed was such that private business would find it too risky, requiring too much capital, or involving too long a payoff period to invest its capital in them. Third, many of the smaller public corporations were created for the hidden purpose of increasing the second-career (amakudari) employment opportunities for retiring higher bureaucrats. (Three-quarters of the top jobs in public corporations are occupied by retired ministerial officials.[2])

Public corporations vary greatly in size. The two supercorporations are the Japan National Railways and the Japan Telegraph and Telephone Public Corporation. With 432,000 and 308,341 employees in 1975, respectively, they are two of Japan's largest employees. They are followed by the Japan Monopoly Corporation (41,097 employees), the Japan Broadcasting Corporation (16,441), and the Metropolitan Area Rapid Transit Authority (10,044). Nineteen others have a staff size of between 1,000 and 10,000 persons, while thirty-two have a staff of less than 100 employees.[3]

Each public corporation is closely identified with a ministry. The corporation is subject to control and supervision of the ministry in operational, budgetary, and personnel matters. The numbers of public and special corporations assigned to ministries and agencies as of January 1, 1975, were as follows: MITI (27), Agriculture (19), Finance (16), Transportation (14), Education (10), Health and Welfare (10), Construction (10), Science and Technology Agency (7), Labor (6), Posts and Telecommunications (5), National Land Agency (4), and the Local Autonomy Ministry (4).[4]

In the Japanese terminology, public corporations are designated variously as kosha, koko, kodan, jigyodan, etc. Although corporations in each category share certain common characteristics, they are not always totally similar. Neither is there a systematic explanation of these terms in the literature. Several important forms of public corporations are identified in the following subsection with brief descriptions of their features.

In order to facilitate their recognition, unofficial English translations of different designations are supplied in quotation marks.

"Public Service" Corporation (*kosha*). After World War II, three of the major economic activities of the national government were transferred from ministries to the newly created public corporations called *kosha*. In 1949, the Japan Monopoly Corporation (JMC, *Nihon Senbai Kosha*) was created out of the Monopoly Bureau of the Ministry of Finance.[b] In the same year, the Japan National Railways (JNR, *Nihon Kokuyu Tetsudo*) was separated from the Transportation Ministry. In 1952, the Japan Telegraph and Telephone Public Corporation (JTTPC, *Nippon Denshin Denwa Kosha*) became independent of the Ministry of Posts and Tele-communications.

Among the different types of public corporations, the kosha is the closest in character to a government department. Kosha are totally owned by the government, and they enjoy a monopoly power in their respective markets. Unlike government departments, however, kosha (as all other public corporations) are on a profit and loss basis; that is, they must pay their way. The budgets of kosha must be approved by the Diet, and their operational plans are deliberated in the Diet along with their budget proposals. Their net earnings must be accumulated as a revolving fund. Their presidents are appointed by the cabinet (JNR and JTTPC) or by the competent minister (JMC). They must obtain the approval of the Diet or the competent minister before they can revise their prices or rates. Borrowing of funds in any form (short-term, long-term, or issuance of bonds) requires an approval of the competent minister.

"Construction and Development" Corporation (*kodan*). There are sixteen "construction and development" corporations, all of which are called *kodan* except the Metropolitan Area Rapid Transit Authority which carries its prewar designation of *eidan*. Of the sixteen such corporations, those which have more than 1,000 employees are, in the descending order of size: Metropolitan Area Rapid Transit Authority, Japan Highway Corporation, Japan Housing Corporation, Japan Railway Construction Corporation, Water Resources Development Public Corporation, and Tokyo Expressway Public Corporation.

The functions of kodan are primarily in the areas of construction and regional development. They make large-scale investments in public housing, roads, irrigation projects, and forestry and water resource developments. Unlike kosha, which operate on a national scale as a monopoly, many kodan are regional in their operation. Initially, kodan capital was

---

[b]Monopoly of salt and tobacco.

fully subscribed by the government. As they developed, however, they came to accept capital participation of local governments. The following aspects of kodan activities require approvals of the competent minister: the budget, the annual operational plans, the disposition of profits, borrowing of all kinds, and the change of prices and rates.

"Project" Corporation (*jigyodan*). There are twenty *jigyodan*. The largest four which had more than 1,000 employees in January 1975 are: Labor Welfare Corporation, Employment Promotion Corporation, Post Office Life Insurance and Annuities Corporation, and Overseas Technical Cooperation Corporation. While kodan deal primarily with construction and development projects, jigyodan undertake various other social and economic activities. As a rule, they are smaller in scale than kodan, and generally lack a business or commercial character. Many "project" corporations are solely owned by the government, but some have their capital subscribed jointly by local authorities or private interest.

"Loan and Finance" Corporation (*koko*). A *koko* is a public corporation which provides supplementary credit to specific areas of economic activity where private financing is insufficient. Its capital is totally subscribed by the government, and the rates of interest it charges on its loans are politically determined (either by the Diet or by the competent minister). As in the case of kosha, the budget of a koko must be approved by the Diet. With an approval of the competent minister, it can raise funds by issuing bonds. Surplus, if any, must be turned over to the Treasury.

There are ten public corporations of loan and finance, which are: People's Finance Corporation; Small Business Finance Corporation; Housing Loan Corporation; Agriculture, Forestry and Fishery Finance Corporation; Small Business Credit Insurance Corporation; Hokkaido-Tohoku Region Development Finance Corporation; Okinawa Development Finance Corporation; Medical Facilities Finance Corporation; Finance Corporation for Local Public Enterprises; and Environmental Sanitation Finance Corporation.[c]

Special Public Banks. A special public bank can be defined as a bank which is created by the government for special purposes and which does not assume the joint-stock form. There are two such banks: the Japan Development Bank (*Nippon Kaihatsu Ginko*) and the Export–Import Bank of Japan (*Nippon Yushutsunyu Ginko*). The functions of these two banks will be discussed in Chapter 9.

---

[c]The financing activities of the loan and finance corporations will be discussed in Chapter 10.

Other Public Corporations. In addition to the fifty-one public corporations discussed above, there are forty-seven other organizations that can also be called public corporations. They are formed under a variety of designations including funds (*kikin*), associations (*kyokai*), and institutes (*kenkyusho*). The largest five with more than 1,000 employees are: Japan Broadcasting Corporation, Social Insurance Medical Fee Payment Fund, Japan Atomic Energy Research Institute, Japan Horse Racing Association, and Electric Measurement Instrument Inspection Center. All these corporations are established by the authority of special laws. The degree of government control over their activities, budgetary and personnel policies and the degree of dependence on public treasury, vary widely from organization to organization.

Special Private Banks and Corporations

The ninety-eight public corporations discussed thus far are essentially public institutions in a legal sense, whether or not they accept participation of private capital. In addition to them, there are fourteen other organizations that are technically private institutions (two cooperatives and twelve joint-stock companies) but are nevertheless regarded as national public enterprises because they are created by special acts of the Diet to serve specific social objectives.

Special Private Banks (*kinko*). The two special private banks are: the Shoko Chukin Bank (*Shoko Kumiai Chuo Kinko*) and the Norin Chukin Bank (*Norin Chuo Kinko*).[d] These are special banks for cooperatives and trade associations. They accept deposits from their member organizations, and make loans to them. They are also empowered to issue debentures to raise loanable funds. The functions of these banks will be discussed in Chapter 9.

Although it is not customary to include the Bank of Japan—the nation's central bank—in public enterprises because of its private origin, it may very well be considered as a special private bank and public enterprise because of the very public role it now plays. Certainly, governmental control over its operations is tighter than control over many public corporations.

Special Private Corporations. Special corporations are joint-stock companies that are established by special laws. As a rule, the capital of these

---

[d]These banks were formerly known in English as the Central Bank for Commercial and Industrial Cooperatives and the Central Cooperative Bank for Agriculture and Forestry, respectively.

corporations are heavily subscribed by the government, and they are under strict governmental supervision. They must pursue the objectives stated by the law, and must obtain the approval of the competent minister on their operational plans, disposition of profits, issuance of debentures, and changes in prices and rates. These firms are established in the areas where private capital is reluctant to get into. The government, therefore, provides the special corporations with guaranteed or protected markets, and gives assistances of subsidies and loans if necessary.

The five largest of the twelve special corporations, in the descending order of size, are: Japan Air Lines Co., International Telecommunication Co., Electric Energy Development Co., Okinawa Electric Co., and Tohoku Development Co. The remaining seven are all small; their personnel number from 30 to 100.

Advisory Councils

The Nature and Characteristics

A large number of advisory councils and commissions are attached to various ministries and agencies. In 1975, there were 246 of them, of which 193 were called *shingikai* (deliberation councils), and others were variously labeled *shinsakai* (examining or qualitying boards), *kyogikai* (conference boards), *chosakai* (study commissions), and *iinkai* (committees).[5] A great majority of these commissions are consultative organs whose function is to study the questions posed by the minister and return reports or recommendations to him. The primary functions of some councils are to render opinions on important licensing applications or on proposed changes in rates and prices. About 10 percent of the commissions perform judicial or supervisory functions. They deal with case-by-case judgment of qualifications, applications, or appeals: Some of them are essentially boards of appeals (e.g., the Pollution Victims Compensation Appeal Board and the Import Duties Appeals Board). Others supervise qualifying examinations and grant licenses (e.g., the Public Accountancy Council and the Veterinary Council).

Each council is administratively attached to a ministry or agency. A section with the ministry serves as secretariat for the council, providing clerical, statistical, research, and editorial work. The Prime Minister's Office has the largest number (51) of councils. Other ministries that have a large number of councils are: MITI (36), Health and Welfare (25), Agriculture and Forestry (24), Finance (20), Education (18), Labor (15), and Transportation (12).[6]

The smallest council has three members, while the largest (the Industrial Structure Council) has 130. The membership of most councils is divided into three broad categories. First, most councils have some government officials representing functionally related ministries. Second, almost all the councils have "persons of learning and experience" (*gakushiki keikensha*). Some members in this category are experts in the relevant field, while others are nonexpert representatives of public interest. A large number of academics are represented in this category. Third, there are members representing all the important constituencies involved in the particular issue. In some cases, members in this category are members of the Diet representing the interests of business, labor, agriculture, or consumer groups.

Selection of council members is made almost exclusively by the officials of the associated ministry. Naturally, only those persons whose views are congenial to the ministerial positions are selected. Antiestablishment individuals and persons who are known to be critical of the government are seldom included. Although membership on most councils involves no remuneration, government officials have little difficulty in finding eager volunteers because of the substantial prestige associated with being a member of these commissions.

The roles played by advisory councils in the government decision-making process may be summarized as follows. In a great majority of cases, their deliberations provide convenient window dressing whose function is to lend respectability to predetermined government positions. Important decisions are made behind the scenes in close and frequent consultations between government officials, business leaders, and the ruling party bosses. The councils often become spokesmen for bureaucratic interests, and, in the worst cases, their recommendations may even serve as whitewashing. Not that all council members are willing sycophants of the government. The complexity of the problems, however, often makes an in-depth study of any given issue difficult. Besides, the mechanism of council meetings does not usually allow ordinary members to make meaningful inputs.

Ministerial officials first define the issue for the council. They provide a preliminary position paper supported by data. The current and former bureaucrats, in close cooperation with the officials of the ministry, effectively steer the direction of council meetings. In due course, the ministerial officials draft the council's report to the minister. In most cases, therefore, the council's final recommendations do not differ fundamentally from the initial government position. However, in some cases where short-run, partisan interests are not involved, council members may be left relatively free of bureaucratic interferences. The intellectual and expert members of the commission may then play a decisive role in shaping the character and quality of the council's deliberations. Its independently reached conclusions, as reported by the mass media, may establish a frame of reference for public debate which may ultimately affect the government decision. In some other cases, a council may provide a forum for debate between the opposing constituencies of a given issue. Conflicting demands of the major elements are reconciled within the commission. When the opposing sides cannot reach an agreement, the "neutral" members of the commission may serve as a final arbiter. The degree of ministerial influence on the neutral members may vary from council to council.

In what follows we examine the character, organization, and workings of four of the more important advisory councils which are charged with the task of advising the government in its economic policy making.

The Economic Council

The Economic Council (*Keizai Shingikai*) is administratively attached to the Economic Planning Agency. The functions of the council are to "study and deliberate on the formulation of long-term economic plans and other important economic policies and programs upon request of the prime minister, as well as to state its opinions, as needed, to the prime minister concerning the same."[7]

The council's membership consists of thirty "persons of learning and experience" serving two year terms. The membership list as of January 1975 was as follows: twelve heads[e] of private corporations (including three heads of banks and one head of a security company), five university professors, five heads of research and consumer organizations, three heads of public corporations, three labor union officials, one advisor to the Foreign Minister, and the vice-governor of the Bank of Japan.[8]

Unlike the scores of smaller and less significant advisory commissions, the Economic Council (as well as a few other key councils) has in its membership some of the topmost leaders of Japan's industrial and financial circles (*zaikai*). For example, the January 1975 membership included the following influential persons:

K. Kikawada (chairman of the council): Board chairman, Tokyo Electric Power Co.; manger, Japan Committee for Economic Development (*Keizai Doyukai*).
S. Nagano: Honorary board chairman Nippon Steel Corporation; president, Japan Chamber of Commerce and Industry (*Nissho*).

---

[e]"Heads" include board chairmen, presidents, vice-presidents, and managing directors.

Y. Iwasa: Board chairman, Fuji Bank; vice-president, Federation of Economic Organizations (*Keidanren*).

Government officials naturally treat a high-powered advisory council such as this with respect and circumspection.

Since the Economic Council was established in 1952, eight long-range national economic plans have been drawn up by the EPA, deliberated by the council, and adopted by the cabinet as basic guiding principles for managing the national economy. They are:

1. Five-Year Plan for Economic Self-Support, 1956–1960.
2. New Long-range Economic Plan, 1958–1962.
3. National Income Doubling Plan, 1961–1970.
4. Medium-term Economic Plan, 1964–1968.
5. Economic and Social Development Plan, 1967–1971.
6. New Economic and Social Development Plan, 1970–1975.
7. Basic Economic and Social Plan, 1973–1977.
8. Economic Plan for the First Half of the Showa 50s (1976–1981).[f]

A brief discussion of the nature of Japanese economic planning follows [9]

In formal terms, an economic plan is prepared by the Economic Council and submitted to the prime minister as a report of the council. In practice, the bulk of the work is done by the officials of the Economic Planning Agency. The preparation of a new plan begins with the prime minister posing a question to the council. For example, in requesting the preparation of the New Economic and Social Development Plan, 1970–1975, the prime minister asked the following question: What should be the nature of the new economic and social plan that could foster a balanced growth of the economy and promote a fuller national life? The question itself implies a great deal about the drift of the plan to be drawn up. In fact, the question is formulated by the EPA, and the agency had already drawn up a draft plan when the question was posed to the council.

The council's work begins formally with the receipt of the request from the prime minister. The plenary council deliberates on the overall framework of the plan. Details are worked out by various subcommittees whose expert members, numbering about two hundred, are recruited temporarily for the task which normally lasts a few months. Although the technical details of the plan are worked out by the EPA officials, the main thrust and orientation of the plan are inevitably colored by the wishes and

[f]The years are fiscal years. The Japanese fiscal year starts on April 1.

values of the powerful zaikai members on the council. As the work progresses, the EPA officials engage in frequent consultations with the officials of other ministries and agencies whose interests are involved. The key ministries such as Finance and MITI have virtual veto power over the content and drift of the plan. Any controversial matters on which ministries cannot agree are kept out of the plan. The final plan—the result of these interministerial consultations and further deliberations by the council—is a statement of what the key officials of the Japanese government and the zaikai leadership jointly consider as the desirable and acceptable new directions of the Japanese economy. The final plan is submitted to the cabinet by the Economic Council and adopted officially with no modification.

The national economic plan is basically a public statement consisting of (1) strategic policy objectives, (2) a set of forecasting of macroeconomic variables such as gross national product, price levels, balance of payments, income distribution, etc., and (3) projections of public investments. Incorporated in the plan are the plans and programs developed by various agencies and ministries: for example, the Land Agency's land development program, the MITI's energy plan, the Transportation Ministry's railroad and highway construction plans, and the Japan Housing Corporation's public housing plan.

Strategic policy objectives vary from plan to plan. The objectives of the 1973–77 plan, for example, were: (1) creation of rich environment, (2) promotion of comfortable and stable national life, (3) achievement of price stability, and (4) improvement of Japan's international economic relations. Policy measures to be used to achieve these objectives are not specified.

The Japanese national economic plan is nonoperational. It is not binding on any party. Targets and projections are not divided for industries or regions. Nor is the EPA equipped with enforcement powers of its own. Each ministry goes its own way implementing its plans. To put it bluntly, Japan's economic planning is an intellectual exercise in forecasting seasoned with wishful thinking. The EPA engages in this exercise, and the Economic Council applies cosmetics to the end product.

The only operational significance of the plan lies in its role as an indicator of the general direction of public policy. Especially of interest to the business community is the direction of public investment planning. Recent five-year plans have revealed a gradual shift of emphasis from economic growth to social welfare. A comparison of the latest plan with the preceding plan shows that the proportion of public investment in the area of social services (environmental improvements, social welfare, and education) in total projected investment increased from 16 percent to 19 percent, while the proportion of investment in transportation decreased from 34 percent to 32 percent.[10] Information of this sort is highly valuable to corporate planners, for it provides important benchmarks for their own planning and projections.

The Industrial Structure Council

The Industrial Structure Council (*Sangyo Kozo Shingikai*, or *Sankoshin* for short) is administratively attached to the Industrial Policy Bureau of the MITI. Its function is stated as follows: "Upon request of the Minister of International Trade and Industry, the council shall study and deliberate on important matters concerning the structure of industry."[11]

The council has a maximum authorized membership of 130 "persons of learning and experience," serving two-year renewable terms and working in eighteen subcommittees. The membership list of January 1975 included twenty-three heads of industrial and trade organizations, sixteen heads of private corporations, fifteen university professors, seven heads of research and consumer organizations, five heads of public corporations, five heads of banks, two heads of local governments, and one labor union official, among others. The council was chaired by T. Doko, the president of the powerful Federation of Economic Organizations (*Keidanren*).[12]

With the collaboration of scholars and business leaders, the MITI officials formulate its industrial policy, and implement it through the industrial bureaus by means of administrative guidance. *Sankoshin* provides a forum for such collaboration. As such, Sankoshin is comparable to the Economic Council. What the Economic Council is to the EPA, the Industrial Structure Council is to the MITI. Both teams—the EPA-cum-Economic Council and the MITI-cum-Sankoshin—engage in economic planning. They both provide a broader policy vision and chart a future course of the national economy. One obvious difference is that while the EPA and the Economic Council concern themselves with the economic life of Japanese society as a whole, the Sankoshin and the MITI focus their attention on the pattern of development of manufacturing and mining industries, commerce, and foreign trade. Another important difference is that while the EPA has no enforcement powers, the MITI enjoys significant regulatory powers over industries and firms.

In the late 1950s and throughout the 1960s the MITI pressed forward what came to be known as the policy of "heavy and chemical industrialization" (*jukagaku kogyoka*). The objective of this policy was to increase the proportion of heavy industrial goods (i.e., machinery and chemical products) in national output and exports. These goods are known to have generally high income elasticity of demand.[g] Increasingly greater specialization in products of higher income elasticity of demand meant that as the world's incomes rose, demands for Japanese products increased proportionally faster. The success of this policy resulted in sharp rises in Japan's exports. Increased earnings of foreign exchanges were ambitiously poured into those industries that promised even faster growth in output and exports. To be sure, other favorable factors—the high domestic saving ratio, the abundance of cheap and high-quality labor, the ready accessibility to foreign technologies, the relatively small defense burden, and the undervalued yen—contributed significantly to the rapid growth of the Japanese economy during the 1950s and 1960s. But without the far-sighted policy by the MITI—allocating scarce resources to high priority areas, promoting the development of new industries, and easing the burden of retrenchment of declining industries by generous assistances—the growth of the Japanese economy in the 1960s would have been much less spectacular.

In the late 1960s the Japanese came to realize that several adverse developments—notably, increased pollution, rising costs of imported raw materials, and the rising shortages of young workers, among others—had made continued rapid expansion of heavy industries untenable. A need for new directions in industrial development was felt; the topic was widely discussed first by academic economists, and later by government officials and business leaders.

The MITI asked the Industrial Structure Council to study and report to it what the new directions of industrial development for the 1970s should be. In May 1971, the council returned an interim report entitled "International Trade and Industrial Policies for the 1970s." Essentially, the report stated that Japan's future industrial development must be concentrated in the so-called knowledge-intensive industries (*chishiki sangyo*). These industries include computers, aircraft, electronics, information services, and fashions, among others. The common characteristic of these industries is that they require relatively little imported raw material, are skill intensive, pollute little, and have generally high income elasticity of demand.

Advisory Councils and Public Pricing

In 1972 there were twenty-six prices and rates that were publicly determined in one way or another. These included the prices of rice, postage

---

[g]The income elasticity of demand is defined as the ratio of the percentage change in the quantity of a product demanded to the percentage change in income. If, for example, the demand for a product increases by 20 percent, while national income rises by 10 percent, the income elasticity of demand for the product is 2.

rates, utilities rates, and the National Railways basic tariff rates. These public prices and rates constitute about 17 percent of the consumer price index. Some of these rates are determined by advisory councils. We examine below how the train fare schedules and the health insurance medical service rates are determined, respectively, by the Transportation Council and the Central Social Health Insurance Council.[13]

The Transportation Council. The Transportation Council (*Un'yu Shingikai*) is advisory to the Minister of Transportation. One of its main functions is to recommend to the minister the size of the annual increase in the basic fare rates of the National Railways. The seven-member council has as an ex officio member the administrative vice-minister of the Transportation Ministry. The other six positions have been traditionally allocated as follows: three to former bureaucrats of the ministry, one to a person representing the legal profession, and the remaining two are shared by the ruling party and the minority parties. Unlike members of many other advisory councils, these six members of the Transportation Council are paid a salary comparable to that of a vice-minister.

The council has been nicknamed the "Tunnel Council," since it has a habit of readily approving government proposals with few modifications. It would be unlikely for the council to make a drastic change in a government proposal, since that would cause havoc in the budgetary process of the government. An official of the Transportation Ministry once stated that for the very reason that the minister had always accepted the council's recommendations without modifications, the council members felt obligated not to submit a recommendation that could not be carried out in practice.[14] Here we see an example of an advisory commission whose main concern is not to embarrass or inconvenience the ministry it advises. Japan's ubiquitous "insider psychology" is at work again. Instead of a citizens' advisory council checking on the behavior of government officials in the public interest, we find an advisory council largely staffed with "insiders" exercising self-restraint in the interest of bureaucratic expediency.

The Central Social Health Insurance Council. The main function of the Central Social Health Insurance Council (*Chuo Shakai Hoken Iryo Kyogikai* or *Chuikyo* for short) is to set the rates for medical services as an advisory to the Ministry of Health and Welfare. In Japan, most medical services are rendered under the various health insurance programs administered by the government. Virtually everyone is covered by one of these programs. The rates for different types of medical treatment and the prices of drugs are fixed by the government and adjusted upward every so often upon recommendation of the *Chuikyo*.

Two opposing partisan groups are represented on the council. On one side is the coalition of "payers"—employers' associations, enterprise-based health insurance unions, and labor unions. They naturally fight against any sizable increases in medical service fees. On the other side are the "payees"—physicians (represented by the Japan Medical Association, JMA), dentists, clinics, pharmacists, and hospitals who would benefit from increases in the rates. The council has been a battleground for these two opposing forces. Of the twenty members of the council, eight each represent the payers and the payees. The remaining four are "public interest" members. Five of the eight members representing the payees' side are officials of the powerful Japan Medical Association. Thus, the battle in the council usually begins with the JMA initiating a rate-hike offensive. The payers' coalition resists the hike, and the coalition of the public interest members and the officials of the Health and Welfare Ministry play the mediators' role.

In August 1972 medical rates were raised by 13.7 percent. Let us briefly trace the developments leading to this outcome. In August of the previous year, the JMA demanded that the rates be raised by 40 percent. The demand for this unusually large increase was politically motivated. The JMA had long maintained that the insurance–medicine system needed a drastic reform. The 40 percent figure, according to the JMA, was what the medical profession must get in order for it to provide what it considered high quality medical services. The payers' side naturally rejected this demand as out of the question. After a considerable amount of arguing and bickering, the JMA lowered the demand to 31 percent. In October 1971, the payers counterproposed a 10 percent increase in the rates. There was no theoretical basis for this figure. Since the general wage level had risen by about 30 percent and the costs of medical services had increased about 20 percent since the previous rate increase, a 10 percent increase in the rates was considered appropriate. With an equal number of members on both sides, there was an impasse which could be broken only by the public interest members working out a compromise. They and the ministry officials concluded that the rate hike should be somewhere between 10 and 15 percent. They were concerned about possible adverse reactions of the public to a rate increase in excess of 15 percent, which was the average rate of increase of wages in that year. After a considerable amount of tinkering with figures, the neutral members proposed a compromise solution of 13.7 percent rate increase. This figure was ultimately accepted by both sides.

Unlike the "tunnel" Transportation Council that readily approves

government proposals with few modifications, the Chuikyo has its own dynamics that rejects one-sided imposition of governmental preferences. The ministry provides a forum of debate between the two opposing forces, retreats to the background, and lets the two sides fight out the battle. Since the relative power of the two sides is neutralized, effective decision-making power comes to rest with the public interest members. Their decisions, in turn, are influenced to a considerable extent by the views and wishes of the ministerial officials.

Notes

1. *Encyclopaedia Britannica*, 15th ed., Micropaedia, s.v. "Public Enterprises."

2. Marshall E. Dimock, *The Japanese Technocracy: Management and Government in Japan* (New York and Tokyo: Walker/Weatherhill, 1968), p. 70.

3. Administrative Management Agency, *Tokushu Hojin Soran, showa 50-nen ban* [Comprehensive listing of special corporations, 1975] (Tokyo: Ministry of Finance, Printing Bureau, 1975), pp. 307–312.

4. Ibid., pp. 313–315.

5. Administrative Management Agency, *Shingikai Soran, showa 50-nen ban* [Comprehensive listing of advisory councils, 1975] (Tokyo: Ministry of Finance, Printing Bureau, 1975).

6. Ibid., pp. 1–11.

7. Ibid., p. 116.

8. Ibid., pp. 116–117.

9. For further information on the nature and scope of economic planning in Japan, see: Victor D. Lippit, "Economic Planning in Japan," *Journal of Economic Issues* 9 (March 1975): 39–58; and Ryutaro Komiya, "Economic Planning in Japan," *Challenge,* May–June 1975, pp. 9–20.

10. *Nihon Keizai Shinbun*, 31 December 1975.

11. Administrative Management Agency, *Shingikai Soran*, p. 339.

12. Ibid., pp. 339–341.

13. The discussions in this subsection are drawn heavily from Masumi Fukatsu, Yasuhiro Kawada, and Norio Ueda, "Kokyo Ryokin Kettei no Seiji Rikigaku," *Chuo Koron,* April 1972, pp. 152–163.

14. Ibid., p. 155.

6

Business Organization and Decision Making

Forms of Business Organizations

The principal types of business organizations that exist in Japan are:

1. *Kojin kigyo* (single proprietor enterprise)
2. *Hojin kigyo* (juridical person enterprise)
   a) *Gomei kaisha* (partnership)
   b) *Goshi kaisha* (limited partnership)
   c) *Yugen kaisha* (limited liability company)
   d) *Kabushiki kaisha* (joint-stock company)

All four types of *hojin* (juridical person) enterprises are legal entities; they can carry on business in their names, enter into contracts, and sue or be sued. *Hojin kigyo* is usually translated as "corporation." It must be noted that this use of the term "corporation" is much broader than the usage in the United States, where the corporation is an equivalent to the Japanese joint-stock company (*kabushiki kaisha*).

The members of a *gomei kaisha* (partnership) are collectively liable for the company's debts if it becomes insolvent. A member cannot transfer his share in the company unless he has a unanimous consent of the other members. A *goshi kaisha* (limited partnership) is essentially the same as a gomei kaisha, except that it has one or more members whose liability is limited to their capital contribution. A limited liability member may transfer all or part of his capital interest with a unanimous consent of the members with unlimited liability. A limited liability member can neither represent the company nor participate in its management.

A *yugen kaisha* (limited liability company) is similar to a joint-stock company in many ways, but it also has some attributes of a partnership. A member's liability is limited to his capital contribution. The total number of members cannot exceed fifty. A member can freely transfer his shares to any other member(s), but transfer of capital interests to outsiders can be made only in accordance with a set of specific procedures. Members elect one or more directors. Members adopt resolutions at a general meeting by a majority vote, the number of votes of each member being prorated to his capital contribution.

77

The Joint-Stock Company

The joint-stock company (*kabushiki kaisha*) is the most numerous and the most important form of incorporated business in Japan. Its main features resemble those of the U.S. corporation. Book II (Company Law) of the Japanese Commercial Code contains the statutory references for the joint-stock company (Articles 165–456).

Formation

At least seven promoters are required to organize a joint stock company. Only the promoters may make noncash contributions. As soon as the subscribers complete their payments for shares, the promoters must convene the first shareholders' meeting. The directors and auditors must be elected at this meeting.

Capital Structure

A joint-stock company may issue common and preferred shares, either with or without a par value. Shares may be either registered or nonregistered. Convertible shares may be converted into another class upon request by the shareholder. The company cannot restrict or prohibit transfers of shares. The Commercial Code prohibits a joint-stock company to offer debentures in excess of an amount equal to the sum of its capital and reserves. Debentures may be of registered or nonregistered (bearer) type. A convertible debenture may also be issued.

Organizational Structure

Shareholders (*kabunushi*). General stockholders' meetings are called by the directors. At least one meeting per year is required; companies that operate on a six-month fiscal period must hold two meetings per year. Shareholders representing one-half of the total common shares outstanding constitute a quorum. Ordinary resolutions are made by a simple majority; certain important matters require a two-thirds majority. Voting by proxy is permitted. Up to one-quarter of the outstanding shares may be preferred stocks without voting rights.

Directors (*torishimariyaku*). A board of directors must have at least three members. Directors are elected at a general shareholders' meeting. The Commercial Code does not permit the article of incorporation to require that a director must also be a stockholder. One or more "representative directors" (*daihyo torishimariyaku*) elected from among the directors may represent the company to the third parties. The Code does not provide for officers of a joint-stock company, except that Book I of the Code states that a merchant (*shonin*) may employ a manager (*shihainin*) to whom the authority may be delegated (Article 37). Article 260 states that "the board of directors is responsible for conducting the company's business, and for appointing and dismissing the manager."

The term manager (*shihainin*) has now become outdated and is seldom used in a modern Japanese corporation. Instead, directors carry officer titles similar to those used in the United States. The Commercial Code implicitly recognizes these titles as it states, in Article 262, that "the joint-stock company shall be held responsible to the bona fide third persons for the acts performed by directors with such titles as president, vice-president, executive managing director, or managing director that may lead the third persons to believe that these directors are empowered to deal with third persons, whether or not they are in fact so empowered."

Auditors (*kansayaku*). A joint-stock company is required by the Code to have at least one statutory auditor whose function is to examine the financial statements prepared by the directors for submission to the stockholders' meeting, and to present his opinion to the meeting. He is empowered to examine the company's books, assets, and operations, and require the directors to present to him financial reports. The term of office of the auditor cannot exceed one year, but it is renewable. A director or an employee of the company is not eligible to be appointed auditor.

Private Corporations—Some Statistics

In 1973 there were over three million single proprietorships (*kojin kigyo*) and nearly one million corporations (*hojin kigyo*) in Japan. Since the partnerships and the limited liability company are not suitable to large business enterprises that require financing through public offerings, virtually all the commercial and industrial enterprises of consequence are organized as joint-stock companies.

Of the 960,000 corporations that existed at the end of 1972, some 781,000 firms (81 percent of total) had capital of less than 5 million yen ($167,000), and contributed to less than one-fifth of total sales by all firms. In contrast, about 1,400 large corporations (0.14 percent of total), each with capitalization of 1 billion yen ($3.3 million) or more, were responsible for about 36 percent of the total sales.[1]

A 1971 study by the Fair Trade Commission showed that the top 100 nonfinancial corporations (in terms of capital) had 2,818 subsidiaries in which they had more than 50 percent shareholding. The total capital of these parent companies and subsidiaries was nearly 40 percent of the total capitalization of Japan's nonfinancial corporations.[2]

Some of the large Japanese corporations are very large even by the world standard. The 1975 *Fortune* list of the 300 largest industrial companies outside the United States included 74 Japanese firms, followed by 53 British firms and 46 West German corporations. Table 6–1 lists the 13 ranking Japanese industrial companies that had sales in excess of $3 billion in 1974. Worldwide, 115 corporations (58 in the U.S. and 57 outside the U.S.) had sales exceeding $3 billion. Thirteen U.S. corporations had sales larger than those of Nippon Steel, the Japanese leader.[3]

The 1975 *Fortune* list of the fifty largest commercial banking companies outside the United States included fifteen Japanese banks, followed by Germany's nine and Britain's five. When we include the U.S. banks, we note that thirteen of the world's fifty largest banks are Japanese, as compared to eleven of the United States and seven of Germany.[4] Table 6–2 lists the ten leading Japanese banks with 1974 assets exceeding $20 billion.

Characteristics of Corporate Organization

We saw earlier in the chapter that the joint-stock company is the most common form of business in Japan. Especially of interest to us is the

Table 6–1
Thirteen Largest Japanese Industrial Corporations, 1974, Ranked by Sales

Rank Outside the U.S.	Rank in the World	Corporations	Sales ($ million)
7	20	Nippon Steel	$8,844
18	37	Hitachi	6,183
19	38	Toyota Motor	5,948
21	41	Mitsubishi Heavy Industries	5,665
27	54	Nissan Motor	4,934
28	56	Matsushita Electric Industrial	4,838
32	64	Nippon Kokan	4,583
36	71	Idemitsu Kosan	4,345
39	74	Sumitomo Metal Industries	4,152
41	76	Tokyo Sibaura Electric	4,117
44	80	Kawasaki Steel	3,892
49	89	Kobe Steel	3,585
50	91	Mitsubishi Chemical Industries	3,563

Source: "The Fortune Directory of the 500 Largest Industrial Corporations," *Fortune,* May 1975, pp. 208–229; "The Fortune Directory of the 300 Largest Industrial Corporations Outside the U.S.," *Fortune,* August 1975, pp. 155–161.

Table 6–2
Ten Largest Japanese Banks, 1974, Ranked by Assets

Rank Outside the U.S.	Rank in the World	Banks	Assets ($ million)
2	5	Dai-ichi Kangyo Bank	$35,727
7	10	Sumitomo Bank	31,063
8	11	Fuji Bank	30,978
9	12	Mitsubishi Bank	29,337
10	13	Bank of Tokyo	28,960
11	14	Sanwa Bank	28,531
16	21	Industrial Bank of Japan	23,189
18	23	Tokai Bank	22,498
20	26	Mitsui Bank	21,755
22	29	Taiyo Kobe Bank	20,331

Source: "The Fortune Directory of the Fifty Largest Commercial-Banking Companies," *Fortune,* July 1975, pp. 116–117; "The Fortune Directory of the Fifty Largest Commercial-Banking Companies Outside the U.S.," *Fortune,* August 1975, pp. 164–165.

internal management organization of large corporations, for they account for the bulk of Japan's productive activities. We also saw that the Japanese joint-stock company resembles the U.S. corporation in its legal framework. In this section we examine the characteristics of the internal management organization of the Japanese joint-stock company. We conclude that, notwithstanding the apparent similarity in form, the organizational behavior of the Japanese corporation is much different from that of the U.S. corporation.[5]

The Familial Traits

In Chapter 2 we observed that the merchant house of Tokugawa Japan was a community in which members were organically related to each other as in a biological family. The familial traits of the Tokugawa merchant house are still observed to a significant extent in the modern Japanese corporation, regardless of its size. The Japanese company is above all a community characterized by primary-group relations among its members. The employees are not considered as outsiders who are selling their labor services to the company on a contractual basis. Rather, they are members of the corporate family, "born " into the family and promoted to higher positions as they grow in age and experience. Care is taken not to disturb the hierarchy of senior–junior relations determined by the employees' years of entry.

The principle of Japanese management organization is one of organizing *people* rather than *work*. The basic unit in Japanese corporate organization is a cluster of people (e.g., a section) who are jointly responsible for the vaguely defined functions assigned to the cluster. Each cluster is headed by a head (*cho*) who reports to the head of a larger cluster. These clusters form a pyramid, reaching the board of directors and the company president at the top. Individuals in the clusters and beyond are tied together organically as in a family. Thus, to a young staff member of a section, the section chief is a father figure, the department head is a grandfather figure, and so on. (The senpai–kohai and oyabun–kobun relations complement the formal vertical ties of the superior and the subordinate. See Chapter 2.) The internal corporate hierarchy of successively higher positions from the subsection chief to president does not, as it does in the West, consist of a series of positions to be filled by interchangeable human actors who qualify for the specific tasks to be performed. Rather, it represents the hierarchy of generations, seniority, and authority of the particularistically related members of a corporate family.

The Bureaucratic Orientation

Japanese corporations, particularly larger ones, exhibit organizational structure and behavior which are characteristic of government bureaucracy. We observed in Chapter 4 that the national government bureaucracy has the following features: (1) The emphasis on formal educational qualifications for entry into the service, (2) the separate tracks (career and noncareer) based on the entrants' educational background, and (3) the importance attached to the year of entry and seniority. These features, which are not unusual for bureaucratic organizations like the civil service or the military, may be considered peculiar when they are adopted by private business firms. Since most of these practices are aspects of the employment system, we will defer their examination to the next chapter. In the remainder of this chapter, our attention will be focused on the structure of management organization and the nature of decision making that takes place in that structure.

The Top Management

Earlier in the chapter we found that the legal frameworks of the Japanese joint-stock company and of the U.S. corporation are quite similar. The use of the board of directors as a trustee of the stockholders' interests is identical under the U.S. and the Japanese corporate laws. The phenomenon of separation of ownership and control is also a conspicuous feature of corporations in both countries. The shareholders' meetings in Japan, as well as in the United States, are usually mere rituals where resolutions predetermined by the management are passed perfunctorily. Voting by proxies often ensures that the top management has enough votes to perpetuate itself.

There are, however, a few significant differences between the management styles of the two countries. First, a typical Japanese board of directors has few outside members. The insider–outsider psychology asserts itself to reject external interferences with the management prerogatives. The corporate community, in the Japanese view, must be controlled by its own members. External directors, when accepted, are usually limited to members of related enterprises. For example, the president of a subsidiary may sit on the board. Or, an officer of the parent company or of the keiretsu bank may serve on the board (see Chapter 8). More often than not, an outside board member serves as a full-time director with managerial duties, usually being dispatched from his organization on a shukko basis.

Second, directorship is regarded as a rank which successful managers can expect to attain with seniority and competence. This is notwithstanding the spirit of the law designating it as trusteeship of shareholders' interests. Division chiefs, and in some cases department heads, are often given the title of director. Persons so designated are generally called "executives" (juyaku). They enjoy special privileges, including exemption from the requirement of the regular retirement age.

The executive lineup of a typical Japanese corporation may look as follows:

Director — board chairman
Director — president
Director — vice-president
Executive managing director(s)
Managing directors
Director — plant manager
Director — sales department head
etc.

Typically, a large Japanese corporation has between twenty and thirty directors. In a corporation with a large number of directors, most directors are naturally junior executives with such functional positions as department heads or managers of branch offices or plants. The Japanese board of directors is therefore not a committee of equals but a group consisting of the company's senior officers of unequal ranks. In view of the traditional rank consciousness, it is natural that decision making in a board of directors is not done by a majority rule. In fact, very little substantive decisions are made by this body.[6]

The real locus of decision making in a Japanese corporation is the executive committee (*jomukai*) consisting of the directors of managing director (*jomu-torishimariyaku*) rank and above. Typically, such a committee consists of five to ten members, including the president (who is usually the board chairman), one or two executive managing director(s) (*senmu-torishimariyaku*), and several managing directors. In some companies the board chairmanship is assumed by a retired president. The extent to which the board chairman wields power, of course, varies from company to company. Customarily, the company president, the board chairman, and one or two more senior officers are designated as representative directors who can legally represent the company to outsiders.

Managing directors, and in some cases even the executive managing director(s), may have responsibility in functional areas such as marketing, manufacturing, and finance. In each of these areas there normally is a line officer who is responsible for managing the daily activities of the department. Such an officer may himself be an ordinary director. There is, however, a subtle difference between the two levels of directors. Senior directors are senior administrators of the corporation, with an added responsibility in a functional area (e.g., managing director in charge of marketing). Junior directors are primarily managers of a department or a division who have been given a title of director (e.g., head of the marketing department with the rank of director).

As stated earlier in the chapter, the Commercial Code requires that a joint-stock company appoint inside auditor(s). In practice, auditors have little work to do; nor much knowledge of accounting is required of them, since the company's books are formally audited by a certified public accountant as required by the Security Exchange Law. Consequently, the position of a statutory auditor has become in most companies a sinecure for a retired senior executive.

Management Organization and Decision Making

So far in this chapter we have seen that Japanese corporate organization is structured primarily as organization of people, rather than of work. How, then, is work organized? How are decisions made in such a structure? This section deals with these questions. We will see that the Japanese management style is strongly influenced by the traditional cultural traits of Japanese society that we discussed in Chapter 2—familism, groupism, rank consciousness, and the vertical interpersonal relations. The discussion in this section is applicable to all types of Japanese bureaucratic organization, both private and public.

Work as a Group Effort

Western management principles regard a firm as consisting of a series of positions (loci of work) to be occupied by qualified specialists. The basic unit of work in an American corporation, for example, is a specialist-manager and his secretary, with perhaps a few assistants. In a Japanese firm, the approach is entirely different. The firm as a collectivity has various tasks to perform, which it assigns to different work groups specializing in these tasks. The work assigned to a group becomes the responsibility of the group, but the functions and responsibilities of individuals in the group are ill-defined and diffuse. The individuals in specialized work groups are, as a rule, generalists. The assumption is that members are motivated to behave in the best interest of the group, and it is not necessary to specify who must do what. Job descriptions in a Japanese organization are, therefore, typically those of a section; one seldom finds job descriptions of individuals. Similarly, organization charts show a pyramid of work groups, not of individual positions.

The basic unit of work in a Japanese bureaucratic organization is a section (*ka*). Three or four sections comprise a department (*bu*). There may be upward of twenty sections (or more) in a large corporation. Some large corporations may have divisions (*jigyobu*), which may be branch offices or plants. Larger sections may be divided into several subsections (*kakari*).

A section typically consists of about a dozen to twenty members, and about one-third to one-half of them are normally clerical workers, largely female high school graduates. The management employees, mostly male college graduates, perform the specialized functions of the section. As they advance in their careers, they are transferred from one department to another, acquiring new skills in each new assignment. Management workers, even section chiefs, do not as a rule have private secretaries. Secretarial work is done collectively by the section's female clerks.

The section chief is not an isolated figure placed over the work team to issue edicts. Rather, he takes a direct part in the team's work as an integral part of the group organization. He is the leader of the team, a father figure, who provides a nexus of authority and group unity. Even in the smallest of corporations, the chief's status is high, and he is treated with a degree of formality of language and demeanor by his subordinates. He is addressed not by his name but by his title, as "*kacho-san*" (Mr. Section Chief).

The chief is not necessarily the most competent worker of the team, but he is almost always older than most of his subordinates. Attention was already drawn in Chapter 2 to the need of the Japanese to belong to a group and be tied vertically with superiors with a degree of emotional dependence. This amae syndrome works as a force that cements the closely-knit management organization and strengthens work group solidarity. The chief (the father figure) is expected to satisfy the dependency needs of the junior workers, both inside and outside of work. Dore reports that when asked in a questionnaire which type of section chiefs workers preferred—one who is business-like and makes little extra work demands but cares little about the personal lives of his subordinates, or one who occasionally makes extra work demands to the extent of breaching the rules but would always look after his subordinates' needs even outside of work—a predominantly large proportion (82–85 percent) of the workers chose the latter.[7]

The close personal relations among the workers and their superiors are reinforced by the relative lack of such communication-inhibiting physical structures as private office spaces, cubicles, and partitions in Japanese offices. A typical Japanese company has large open areas filled with desks. Only the high-level executives have private offices. A middle manager, say, a section chief, works side by side with his subordinates. His desk may be adjacent to his subordinates' desks, or may be separated by a few feet. His superior, the department head, also has his desk located in a central position surrounded by clusters of desks belonging to different sections. Often it is difficult for the outsider to tell where one section ends and another section begins. In such a physical surrounding, it is difficult for any manager to conduct business in private or keep distance from his subordinates. The relationship, though formal, is inevitably close and personal.

The close primary-group relations among fellow workers are further fostered by the age-old tradition of drinking and having merriment together. Companies sponsor at their expense one or two overnight trips each year to a resort area for their employees. The whole group stays together in a hotel or an inn. The main event on such an excursion is the dinner and the ensuing drinking and singing party. Most women leave the party and retire to their quarters before the party gives way to too much merrymaking. Even though family members do not usually accompany the employees, sex is strictly a taboo on these trips. The main function of these trips is to unite the men emotionally, and the relaxed atmosphere of the resort area and a lot of *sake* and beer do the job. Besides these excursions, office groups engage in several drinking parties each year, the end-of-year *bonenkai* ("forget-the-year party") being the biggest event. The significance of all these parties is that they help strengthen the solidarity of the work team as an organic community with a high emotive content.

Company-sponsored parties and excursions are but one aspect of the overall corporate efforts to win the employees' loyalty to the company and to generate and maintain harmonious relations among them. Other activities include: frequent ceremonies, training of new recruits with group living, company-run facilities in resort areas for the employees and their families, company-run and subsidized dormitories for single workers, company-subsidized eating facilities, and company-sponsored sports events. Lifetime employment and seniority-based wage and promotion systems are, of course, the two pillars of corporate efforts to win employees' identification with and loyalty to the company.

Rank-Conscious Consensus Formation

As work is a group effort, decision making is also a group activity. The basic principle of the Japanese decision-making process is one of consensus. Deeply ingrained in the Japanese way of thinking is a belief that nothing is black and white, there is no absolute truth, and no person can be absolutely right or wrong. When the Japanese faces a serious problem on which he is asked to take a stand, the first thing he wants to do is to learn the perspectives of others. A person who makes a quick decision and sticks with it is considered rash and immature. The Japanese instinctively seek others' views and adjust their own tentative position to them. This process inevitably involves a series of long and tedious (to the Western observer) meetings and individual consultations. As each participant makes a series of small adjustments to his initial (unpublicized) position, a majority view begins to take shape. The majority seeks to obtain the consent (*nattoku*), if not the agreement, of all or almost all of the participants. Overruling the minority by a 51 percent majority vote is considered uncivilized and disruptive of group harmony. The minority, on the other hand, seldom persists in the unpopular position. As two-thirds or three-quarters of the participants come to agree on an emerging consensus, the remaining minority quickly yields to the majority and gives its consent to the majority position. They are satisfied that their voices are heard and that their views are reflected more or less in the consensus that has emerged. Above all, their faces are saved, they know further persistence is not wise. If overruling a minority view is uncivilized, persisting in the minority position is worse. A maverick who persists in unpopular positions on too many occasions risks losing the acceptance of the group, which is a very serious matter.

Decision making by consensus is facilitated by the differences in the rank or status of the participants. The nature of interpersonal relations in

Japanese organization being as it is, the subordinates make every effort to accommodate to, and even internalize, the values and wishes of their superiors. They do this partly because they recognize that their superiors are more experienced and hence wiser, and partly because they know that loyal cooperation with superiors enhances their chances of promotion in the organization. "Consensus" in Japanese management organization is therefore likely to develop around the views and positions of the persons of authority. The more junior a participant is, the greater the extent to which he accommodates himself to the group position.

This method of arriving at a group decision has some merits as well as some shortcomings. On the merit side, we note that the process is conducive to group harmony, inasmuch as it allows each person to air his views and thereby makes him feel that his views count. This enhances his sense of belonging to the group and strengthens his sense of identification with the organization. When the time comes to implement the chosen solution, there exists the commitment of all concerned to work in harmony toward its successful execution. The Japanese-style decision making can also be said to be "democratic" in the sense that there is little room for a superior to exercise arbitrary authority. If he realizes that many of his subordinates cannot agree with his position, he is not likely to bulldoze them with it. Rather, he is more likely to accommodate his position to their views, since he knows that an effective implementation of the project is not possible without concerted actions of all involved.

On the drawback side, we note first of all that this system is time consuming. Long meetings, endless discussions, and frequent indecisions are the unavoidable by-products of this process. Parenthetically, we might mention that few Japanese managers really "hate those meetings," as do their Western counterparts. The Japanese draws a sense of belonging and participation from these meetings. What the Western manager considers as an inescapable chore, the Japanese manager views as central to his work and life.

The second disadvantage of the Japanese-style decision making is its indecisive nature. If a significant minority remains opposed to a position, and all attempts at persuading it fail, the natural tendency for the group is not to take any action on it. The proposal is tabled, in some cases indefinitely. Indecision is preferred to disruption of group harmony. If a decision cannot be postponed, then less meaningful compromise must be accepted as the only solution. Consensus may thus mean that everybody gets his second best.

Third, there is always a danger that a sound minority view is suppressed prematurely. In the individualistic West, a person of strong conviction would not hesitate to take a strong position against the majority view, and would persist in his criticism of it so that eventually he might succeed in undermining it. In the Japanese social milieu, such an occurrence is rare. The dissenters are quick to sense the group pressure being exerted on them, and waste little time adjusting their position to the majority view. Their emotional dependence on the group is so great that few are able to withstand the group pressure for long. *Fuwa raido* ("me too" syndrome) is a hallmark of Japanese society. Once the wheel starts to turn in one direction, it is difficult to stop it or alter its course, since an internal mechanism for such a move is lacking. This deficiency applies equally to a Japanese social organization and to Japanese society at large.

The "Bottom-Up" Process

In a Japanese bureaucratic organization, lower-level managerial staff members assume a much larger role than their Western counterparts in developing policies and shaping solutions. The workhorses in a large organization are section chiefs, department heads, and their assistants in their late thirties and early forties. In many cases these middle managers actively participate in formulating major policies of the organization. Senior managers are not regarded as issuers of directives that their subordinates must carry out. Rather, they are viewed as facilitators, harmonizers, and motivators. They are expected to create an atmosphere in which subordinates can do creative work on their own initiative.

This does not mean, however, that senior executives are passive fixtures who merely ratify the decisions made by the middle managers. Rather, the top executives participate in the decision-making process by setting a keynote on which all decisions are to be made. The middle managers are well aware of the wishes of their superiors, and they lay them to heart when they formulate their proposals. When a subordinate submits a proposal to the superior, the latter asks questions, makes suggestions, or returns the work to him for further study. When they both agree that the proposal has merit, then the superior submits it to his own superior for evaluation and/or approval. This process is repeated through the echelons of hierarchy from the section chief to the company president.

The procedure of this bottom-up decision making is formalized in the so-called *ringi* system. Ringi can be loosely translated as "proposal submission for deliberation and approval." This system is widely used in the Japanese government bureaucracy and in large corporations. The system works as follows: in an interoffice memorandum called a *ringisho*, a lower-level manager (usually a section chief) details a specific recommendation on a given matter. After it is approved by his immediate superior (say, the department head), the document is circulated among the relevant section and department heads, after which it climbs the hierarchy to the company president. The chief of each section and department that are consulted must affix his seal of approval before the ringisho goes any further. One could refuse to affix his seal and thereby block the upward movement of the proposal, but such an occurrence is rare. If he does not approve the proposal, he is more likely to sit on it without taking any action, thus delaying the circulation of the document. In such a case, some sort of accommodation is often reached between the initiator of the ringisho and the person who has objections. Any executive may return the document to his subordinate for reconsideration or improvement. Once the ringisho is approved by the president and receives his seal, the proposal becomes a company policy.

Although a ringisho is drafted by a junior-level manager, the idea for the proposal may originate at any level. The company president, for example, may suggest an idea to one of his executives, who in turn may convey the idea to a department head and instruct him to have a ringisho developed by one of his section chiefs. In some cases a ringisho is drawn up to place in record or formalize what has already been approved informally in a meeting. In those cases, the ringi is called *ato-ringi* ("after-the-fact" ringi).

The system of ringi thus does not signify a one-way bottom-up flow of initiatives. Rather, it serves as a convenient vehicle that allows and encourages lower-level managers to take the initiative in shaping specific solutions to problems and submitting them upward for approval. Unlike the Western management system, where directives flow predominantly from the top down, in the Japanese system there exist effective two-way flows. The system of ringi provides junior managers an opportunity to make inputs into their company's decision-making process and also to demonstrate their capabilities to their superiors.

While ringi is a well established system, it is not central to the Japanese decision-making process. The essence of the Japanese-style management system is the pattern of activity called *nemawashi*, a process of informal prior consultation, deliberation, and persuasion. It is rare for the initiator of a ringi to circulate the ringisho without first "touching bases" with all the major parties involved. Similarly, a lot of spadework is done by all the involved individuals before a formal meeting on any issue takes place, especially by those who must "sell" an idea or an argument.

The essence of nemawashi is coordination and persuasion, dealing primarily with persons outside one's immediate work group. As such, nemawashi requires skills in interpersonal relations. The practitioners of nemawashi take full advantage of their clique connections and senpai–kohai (senior–junior) and oyabun–kobun (patron–protégé) relations extending beyond their immediate work groups. Equally important are the small "loans" (kashi) and "debts" (kari) accumulated over the years. To sum up: Instead of adopting the Western-style adversary system of decision making, where conflicting positions are resolved ultimately by a majority vote, the Japanese still rely heavily on their tradition-based consensus method that involves a series of face-saving compromises achieved primarily through the channels of interpersonal relations and obligations.

Both ringi and nemawashi involve a considerable amount of upward movement of initiatives. How can this bottom-up process be reconciled with the hierarchy orientation of Japanese society and the rank consciousness of the Japanese people? The answer lies in the nature of interpersonal relations in Japanese social organization. The Japanese subordinate, in submitting a proposal to his superior or criticizing the superior's views, tries to be very diplomatic and differential in his demeanor and language. He is also aware of his superior's wishes and spares no effort in incorporating them in his own proposals and recommendations. More important than the style of delivery, however, is the system of seniority-based promotion in Japanese business and government organizations. The superior, knowing fully well that his subordinates—no matter how bright or competent they may be—cannot surpass him on the ladder of advancement in the organization, does not feel threatened by competent subordinates and hence can accept their recommendations and criticisms with equanimity. On the contrary, a good work by his subordinates is a credit to the quality of his leadership.

On this score, Nakane points out that the required qualification of the leader in Japanese society is not so much his own ability to conduct business as his ability to understand his subordinates, capture them emotionally by his personality, and synthesize and direct their talent. She maintains that it is better for the leader not to be "outstandingly bright," for under such a person the subordinates may become alienated.[8] Henderson succinctly sums up the situation when he says that the Japanese manager is rated for the "followership" that he can induce among his subordinates.[9]

The prevalence of bottom-up process and consensus-based decision making in Japanese social organizations should not be construed as an evidence of the lack of exercise of power by persons of authority. Power *is* exercised, albeit in a uniquely Japanese way. It is exercised by suggestions, by manipulations of group dynamics, and by resort to the sense of *giri*. The superior seldom *orders* the recalcitrant subordinate to mend his ways. Instead, he would *suggest* that his uncooperative behavior may not be in the best interest of the group and may detract from the good standing of the subordinate in the group. Such a suggestion would normally have a very powerful influence on the subordinate's behavior. This is partly because an inferior in Japanese social organization is conditioned to attribute authority to the wishes of his superior, and partly because the subordinate is extremely conscious of his standing in his group. The fear of being rejected by the group is intense, and the person of authority can adroitly manipulate it to achieve his objective.

The threat of group rejection may be effectively combined with the force of giri obligation (see Chapter 2). Often, a subordinate owes giri to his superior. For example, he may be the subordinate's university senpai or even an oyabun. The superior may have in the past been helpful to him in personal or financial matters. In all such cases, the sense of giri on the part of the subordinate makes it difficult for him to say no to the superior's wishes. Wielding of power by persons of authority in Japanese social organizations therefore is just as effective as in the West, albeit it is done differently. The bottom-up process must be understood within this larger context of the hierarchical authority and power relations.

The Goals of Private Corporations

We have thus far examined how decisions are made in Japanese firms. We may now ask for what purposes decisions are made—that is to say, what the goals of Japanese corporations are.

It is axiomatic that the goals of a corporation are to enhance the security, power, prestige, and material well-being of its members. This axiom, however, begs the question of who the members are. In the conventional view, a corporation belongs to its owners, and the employees—including the managers—are mere hired hands who are paid to do the job of maximizing profits for the shareholders. This view, however, has long lost its relevance to reality, especially in the United States and Japan where the so-called managerial revolution has advanced to a very high level. There, corporations belong to their managers—a group of individuals whom John K. Galbraith calls the members of the Technostructure[10]—and the shareholders are regarded as "creditors" from whom the enterprise "borrows" equity capital.[a] Only 6 percent of

---

[a]General shareholders' meetings in most corporations are mere rituals, more so in Japan than in the United States. Professional troublemaker/extortionists called *sokaiya* ("shareholders' meeting specialists") smooth things over and enable the management to complete the meeting eventlessly and quickly, often in less than an hour. Owning only a few shares of stock, they inspect the company's books, attend shareholders' meetings, and ask embarrassing questions and often raise havoc. In return for payments of handsome "fees," they work for the management and heckle and rough up ordinary shareholders who dare demand the floor. Up to half of the people attending a meeting of a large corporation may be sokaiya. According to one estimate, there are some 1,500 sokaiya in the Tokyo area, squeezing over 30 billion yen ($100 million) each year from the 1,600 companies listed on the

the 1,500 Japanese executives included in a 1962 study had achieved their positions through ownership.[11] Even in owner-controlled firms, the owners' interferences with managerial functions tend to be minimized because of the collectivist nature of the Japanese management system. To a greater extent than Galbraith sees in U.S. corporations, the arbitrary interferences of owners are rejected in a successful Japanese corporation. Where such interferences are frequent, the firm cannot function well and is likely to become a failure. Managers who own a significant portion of the corporation's shares must therefore work as cooperative members of the corporate team if they want the firm to be successful.

Galbraith's view of the modern corporation and its goals fits the Japanese case fairly well. He states that a modern corporation is run by committees of specialists/professionals (the Technostructure), and their goals become the corporate goals.[12] This is essentially true in the Japanese case, with a few notable qualifications. First, the "members" of a Japanese corporation include its regular clerical and production workers, although the goals of the corporation tend to reflect those of the managers. Second, as noted earlier, Japanese managers are mostly generalists rather than specialists. Third, because of the rank and seniority consciousness in Japanese social organization, the values and preferences of senior managers tend to weigh more heavily than those of junior managers. It may be safe to conclude that the goals of a typical large Japanese corporation are those of its senior managers. Specifically, we may identify the *jomukai* (executive committee) as the goal-setting organ of the corporation.

In considering the goals of senior executives, two points must be kept in mind. First, as noted in Chapter 2, the Japanese are extremely rank conscious. Enhancing the prestige and rating of their company in the industry and in the nation is naturally utmost in the minds of corporate executives. Second, profit maximization for the "nameless and faceless" stockholders must be ruled out as an important goal of the management. Senior executives in most large Japanese corporations gain little personally from large profits, since the popular American practices of executive stock options and bonuses directly tied to profitability are rather uncommon in Japan.

The primary goal of Japanese corporate management is to maintain a high and rising volume of sales. Growth of corporate output and sales has the following consequences. First, it assures an adequate level of profits. Although *maximization* of profits is not a corporate goal, earning a mini-

---

Tokyo Stock Exchange. See Kenji Ino, "Sokaiya to Kigyo no Atsui Naka," *Bungei Shunju,* August 1973, pp. 350–360. Also see T.F.M. Adams and N. Kobayashi, *The World of Japanese Business* (Tokyo: Kodansha International, 1969), pp. 82–85, for a fairly detailed account of sokaiya activities.

mally acceptable level of profits is. The firm is expected to pay a respectable rate of dividend commensurate with its position in the industry. A failure to do so is an open admission of the ineptitude of the management—a loss of face. Reduced profits and dividends may depress the price of the company's stock—another loss of face. Second, increased volume of sales is considered important because it leads to an increase in the company's share of the market. The share of the market and the company's capitalization are the two most frequently used measures of the size, and hence the rank in the industry, of the company. Third, a high and rising volume of sales means "cheerful life" for everybody concerned. It means more and faster promotions for the managers, higher wages and larger bonuses for all the employees, larger expense accounts for the executives, and more welfare programs and recreational benefits for the workers. Higher levels of cheerfulness are more conducive to the harmony and solidarity of the corporate family. Fourth, growth means a continued high level of employment of its production workers. Because of the custom of tenured employment of regular workers, layoffs and dismissals are difficult, and, if done, costly and demoralizing. Lastly, high and rising levels of sales enable the firm to meet the large interest payments on its typically large external debts (bank borrowings). Failure to keep up with interest payments would invite interferences by banks with the autonomy of the management and the firm.

To say that firms do not consider maximizing profits as their primary goal does not mean that they are indifferent to profits. They naturally prefer more profits to less, other things being equal, as a means of achieving their primary goal, growth.

In 1972–74, during the period of rapidly rising commodity and land prices, some of Japan's largest corporations were seized with a money-grabbing fever. The condition of excess liquidity caused by the huge balance-of-payments surpluses drove some corporations into pouring enormous sums of money into speculative purchases of commodities, stocks, and land. The worst damage to society was done by their wholesale grabbing of land in all parts of the country. In 1973 alone, corporations spent 9.8 trillion yen ($33.3 billion) on land purchases, of which two-thirds were financed with bank loans.[13] Not only real estate, construction, and railway companies, but also some general trading firms and even manufacturing companies participated in this rush. Banks accepted the purchased land as collateral, and thrust more money upon sometimes hesitant corporations. Sharp rises in land prices resulted. In 1974, a small (by the American standard) two-story, three-bedroom house on a sixty-by-sixty-foot lot in a choice Tokyo suburb could easily command upward of 30 million yen ($100,000), two-thirds of which was the cost of the land. A large proportion of Japan's younger generations today have abandoned their hopes of owning a home in their lifetime. The acute housing shortage and the incredibly high prices of land constitute one of Japan's most serious social problems today, and the speculative land purchases of the nation's largest corporations aggravate the situation. This, and the stockpiling of commodities by some general trading firms in the period of acute commodity shortages during 1972–74, revealed a great deal of antisocial character of Japan's big business, and shook severely the confidence and trust the public had had in them.

Many corporate managers pronounce that their firms' activities serve the larger public purpose of economic growth. Consistency of social and corporate goals has made it easier for corporations to declare that their missions are to serve the society beyond their gates. These pronouncements serve several important functions. First, the idealistic posture enhance the prestige of the firm. Profit making for its own sake has always been looked down upon in Japanese society. *Watakushi* (private) in all cases is expected to serve the *oyake* (public). Corporations that portray themselves as public organizations in pursuit of the greater purposes of society acquire a little of oyake character and therefore become more prestigious in the eyes of the public. Second, as Galbraith points out, a high degree of worker identification with the corporation can be achieved when the firm's goal is respectable. A "public-minded" firm can be assured of loyalty and commitment of workers to the extent that is not possible in a pecuniarily motivated firm. Lastly, the firm's public-minded pronouncements enable the management to pressure the workers to make convenient sacrifices for the company in the name of greater social welfare.

In recent years, as the goal of Japanese society has gradually shifted from a maximum output of material things to a more balanced growth with a greater emphasis on the qualities of life, the congruence between societal and corporate goals has diminished markedly. Whether Japanese corporations can continue to pursue the goal of growth in a nongrowth environment, and whether they can maintain their past vitality if they must now abandon growth as their overriding goal, remain to be seen.

Notes

1. Nikkei Business Henshu-bu, *Nihon no Kigyo Kankyo* [The environment of Japanese business] (Tokyo: Nihon Keizai Shinbun-sha, 1974), pp. 14–15.

2. Dan Fenno Henderson, *Foreign Enterprise in Japan: Law and Policies* (Chapel Hill, N.C.: University of North Carolina Press, 1973), p. 129.

3. "The Fortune Directory of the 500 Largest Industrial Corporations," *Fortune,* May 1975, pp. 208–229; "The Fortune Directory of the 300 Largest Industrial Corporations Outside the U.S.," *Fortune,* August 1975, pp. 155–161.

4. "The Fortune Directory of the Fifty Largest Commercial-Banking Companies," *Fortune,* July 1975, pp. 116–117; "The Fortune Directory of the Fifty Largest Commercial-Banking Companies Outside the U.S.," *Fortune,* August 1975, pp. 164–165.

5. For further information on Japanese management organization and decision making, see: M. Y. Yoshino, *Japan's Managerial System: Tradition and Innovation* (Cambridge, Mass.: The MIT Press, 1968); and Ezra Vogel, ed., *Modern Japanese Organization and Decision-Making* (Berkeley and Los Angeles: University of California Press, 1976).

6. Vogel, *Modern Japanese Organization,* p. 121.

7. Ronald Dore, *British Factory, Japanese Factory* (Berkeley and Los Angeles: University of California Press, 1973), p. 237.

8. Chie Nakane, *Japanese Society* (Berkeley and Los Angeles: University of California Press, 1972), p. 65.

9. Henderson, *Foreign Enterprise,* p. 111.

10. John Kenneth Galbraith, *The New Industrial State* (Boston: Houghton Mifflin Co., 1967), chap. VI.

11. Yoshimatsu Aonuma, *Nihon no Keieiso* [The managerial class in Japan], p. 140, cited in Yoshino, *Japan's Managerial System,* pp. 88–89.

12. Galbraith, *The New Industrial State,* chap. XV.

13. *Asahi Shinbun,* 3 March 1976.

7

The Employment System and Industrial Relations

Legacies of the Tokugawa Employment System

Every aspect of Japanese social organization is a reflection of the familial orientation of Japanese society, and the employment relations is no exception. A place of work is a family-like community to the Japanese worker, a community of people organized to achieve a common goal. Within the community exist hierarchical and particularistic relations resembling those in a biological family. A social boundary is drawn around it, and its members depend on each other for emotional support and fulfillment, with a shared sense of indifference or antipathy toward the outsiders.

The prototypes of the Japanese employment system are found in the employment relations of the Tokugawa period. We saw earlier (Chapter 2) that an employee was recruited by a Tokugawa merchant house at an early age as an apprentice and stayed with the house as a second-class family member with his remuneration and rank progressively rising as he grew older and more experienced. The relationship between the employee and the head of the house was diffuse; the latter was frequently involved in the personal life of the worker.

In the craft, somewhat different employment relations existed. The apprentice who acquired the necessary skill would, after completing a customary term of service with his master (*oyakata,* literally a "father figure"), work as a craftsman for other masters who paid him the wage commensurate with his skill. There was thus a labor market where craftsmen's services could be bought and sold at wages that varied in response to the forces of supply and demand. Uninvolved labor markets existed also for various unskilled jobs, such as temporary household services, hauling of goods, and work in the mines, at the docks, and at construction sites. Unskilled labor was often supplied by labor bosses (also called *oyakata*) who provided protection and daily provisions to itinerant day laborers in exchange for a "cut" in their earnings. What these labor contractors could command as wages for their men, of course, varied according to the forces of supply and demand.

When we add, to the above, the employment relations of the samurai and the peasant, we have a virtually complete picture of the Tokugawa employment system. Three rather distinct types of employment structure can be identified: (1) the hereditary lifetime employment of the samurai and the family farming of the peasant, (2) the lifetime employment coupled with the seniority-based reward system of the merchant houses, and (3) the relatively free labor markets of craftsmen and day laborers.

The discussions in this chapter show that the present employment systems of Japan are essentially mixtures of the Tokugawa employment institutions. Two rather distinctly different types of employment relations are identified in Japan today. One is commonly referred to by foreign observers as the "Japanese employment system" (hereafter JES). The distinguishing characteristics of the JES are lifetime employment, wages and promotion based on the workers' length of service, and an elaborate system of fringe benefits. This system is applicable only to public employees and regular workers of large corporations. The other type of employment relations may be called the "market employment system." It applies to the employment relations of the workers of small business firms and the temporary workers of large corporations. What we are dealing with here, of course, is the "dual structure" of the Japanese labor market. According to one estimate, about one-half of Japan's total labor force fell in each type of employment relations in 1970.[1]

In the JES we see direct institutional continuity from the Tokugawa period on two counts. The first—the lifetime employment and the seniority-based reward system—is, of course, derived directly from the practices of the Tokugawa commercial houses. Although originally applied only to employees in the managerial ranks, these practices were extended to blue collar workers after World War I. The second is the rigid differentiation of worker status into three categories—managerial (subdivided into elitist and nonelitist in the government bureaucracy), clerical, and blue collar. In the Tokugawa period, the class differentiation was hereditary, that is, by ascription by birth. In modern Japan, as we observed in Chapter 3, the assignment of worker status is based primarily on reascription by education and examinations.

Temporary workers of large corporations are considered "nonmembers" of the corporate family, and few of the community-like, particularistic benefits or obligations are applicable to them. Their relationship with the company is strictly business—that is, purely contractual and specific in its obligation. This relationship resembles that of Tokugawa craftsmen and day laborers with their employers.

The employment relations of small business firms are basically characterized by free labor markets. Small firms are manned by workers who have been unable to go to good schools or failed in competition for employment in large establishments. Obligations of both employers and employees are specific, wages vary according to skills and market conditions, and fringe benefits are minimum. Unlike temporary workers of large corporations, however, employees of small business firms, especially long-term workers of small family businesses, tend to develop diffuse and personalized relations with their employers which are reminiscent of the master–servant relations of the Tokugawa merchant house. Promotions of long-term employees are likely to be based on seniority and their particularistic relations to the employer. The employer tends to be paternalistic to his employees, while at the same time being meddlesome with the personal life of the workers.

In the remainder of this chapter, our attention is focused primarily on the employment relations of large corporations, particularly those involving regular workers.[2]

The Nature of "Corporate Paternalism"

The virtues of the traditional family ideology of mutual affection, benevolence, and reciprocity are often extolled as the essence of the Japanese employment relations. The widespread practices of lifetime employment, the seniority-based reward system, and the extensive system of fringe benefits in large corporations are often cited as manifestations of "paternalistic" employer–employee relations.

Upon close examinations, however, one finds that truly paternalistic relations—the personal paternalism of the Tokugawa merchant house—exists today only in small, nonunionized family firms. In large corporations, personal paternalism exists only in the interstices of their organization in the form of the personal benevolence of the superior, oyabun, and senpai to their subordinates and juniors.

Having said this, we must be cautioned against drawing an opposite (and unwarranted) conclusion that employment relations in large Japanese corporations are purely impersonal cash nexuses of the market place. What, then, is the exact nature of the so-called corporate paternalism? First, we must recognize that "paternalism" in large corporations is not personal, but institutionalized and contractual. The workers' benefits are institutionalized as their "rights" and distributed to them according to specific rules that are often topics of heated debates in collective bargaining sessions.[3]

Second, it is important to note that job security, seniority-based rewards, and generous fringe benefits for production workers are not the results of humane considerations of management in the welfare of workers. Rather, these practices gradually took hold in large corporations after World War I as calculated responses to the problems of skilled-labor shortage and high labor turnover. Before World War I, skilled male workers were tied particularistically to master workmen (*oyakata*), who provided their services to enterprises as independent labor contractors. The technological requirements of heavy industry, however, made this arrangement obsolete. Firms now needed a stable supply of well-trained and highly skilled in-house workers. In order to induce oyakata and their men to join their firms, managers offered, as incentives, status of full-time employees guaranteed against dismissal. The status hierarchy, personal paternalism, and the wage and employment relations of the oyakata system were thus transplanted to large enterprises.[4] The recent migrants from the rural areas who constituted the bulk of industrial workers found a new type of security in the paternalistic ideology of the firm and the accompanying job security and tangible material benefits.

Whatever its origin and the present ideological billing may be, the significance of "corporate paternalism" today lies in its effects on the workers' morale and motivations. It provides security to workers and strengthens their identification with the company. It helps generate the all-important *wa* (harmony) among the regular and permanent employees. It must be remembered, moreover, that within this larger framework of institutionalized paternalism operates the personal paternalism of section chiefs and foremen. Affective solidarity generated in the subgroups, and the attachment to company generated by the "paternalism" of the company, reinforce each other in helping the workers internalize the values and goals of the corporation.

As an analogy to welfare statism, Dore labeled the nonpersonal paternalism of big Japanese firms "welfare corporatism."[5] This label is somewhat misleading. The company is primarily concerned about the welfare of its regular and permanent members (which, of course, include the top managers) and, to a lesser extent, with that of the regular and semipermanent members. The management is little concerned about the welfare of the temporary workers. "Corporate paternalism" is essentially a welfare-maximizing behavior of the firm's regular and permanent members.

Categories of Worker Status

As we observed in Chapter 3, categories of worker status in large Japanese corporations are determined by the workers' educational background and entrance examination results. Figure 7–1 shows the categories in a summary form. Managerial and technical jobs are limited to university graduates, and clerical and production workers are recruited from among middle and high school graduates. No specific educational qualifications are required of temporary and outside workers. Promotion from one status category to another is rare; when it is done, the promoted employee is treated as a midcareer employee (*chuto saiyosha*) and must suffer the stigma attached to that status.

Regular Employees

Regular employees are *miuchi* (insiders) of the firm, although not all of them are "full" members. They are recruited as a rule from young school

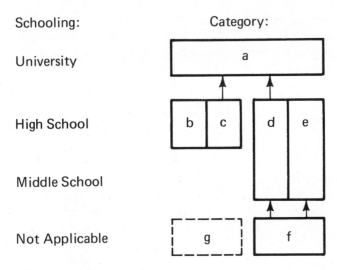

Schooling: Category:

University   a

High School   b   c   d   e

Middle School

Not Applicable   g   f

[a]Managerial and technical employees, predominantly male.

[b]Clerical employees, female.

[c]Clerical employees, male.

[d]Manual workers, male.

[e]Manual workers, female.

[f]Temporary workers.

[g]Outside workers.

> Regular employees = a through e.
>
> Permanent employees = a, c, and d.
>
> Semipermanent employees = b and e.

Arrows indicate status promotion.

Figure 7–1. Categories of Worker Status.

leavers upon passing entrance examinations. They automatically become members of the labor union, and enjoy all the amenities of the firm's welfare facilities. Their wage structure is tied to seniority, or more precisely, to the length of service (*nenko*). They can as a rule count on employment with the firm until they retire.[a] In the cases of clerical and blue collar workers, labor unions, as a policy, limit membership to a size which ensures uninterrupted employment of all regular workers at all times. The company adjusts the size of its total work force to changing business conditions by varying the number of temporary workers. The

---

[a]Most women workers retire at marriage or at first pregnancy. See the discussion on semipermanent employees later in this chapter.

wage and fringe benefit costs of the regular workers of a company thus assume the character of fixed costs. Regular employees are divided into permanent and semipermanent employees.

Permanent Employees

The permanent employees of large corporations are the aristocrats of the Japanese working class. They are the "full" members of the corporate community. There are three categories of workers in this class: (1) managerial workers who are predominantly male university graduates, (2) high school graduates (predominantly male) who start as clerks and retire as lower-middle level managers, and (3) male production workers with middle or high school education. In all three categories, workers are recruited each year from among new graduates of schools and universities and join the firm after passing highly competitive entrance examinations (see Chapter 3). Their employment until retirement is virtually guaranteed. Their ranks and wages are positively correlated with the length of their service.

University graduates can rise from junior managerial positions to the top management, depending on their ability. High school graduates in white collar jobs rise from the lowest-rank clerk position to the lower-middle management position by the time they retire. The larger a corporation is, the sharper in general is the distinction between the managerial (university graduates) and clerical (high school graduates) categories. In the largest of firms, high school graduates seldom rise above subsection chief. In other large firms they may be promoted to section chief. Smaller firms accept both high school and university graduates for undifferentiated clerical/managerial positions. Promotion of high school graduates, however, tends to be at a slower pace. Middle and high school graduates in production jobs are promoted gradually through the ranks to, eventually, supervisor or above, if they are capable. The highest position which a production worker with high school education is likely to reach is subsection chief in a production department.

One unique characteristic of the JES is the parallel existence of two different scales of "rank." Just as in the military, most large corporations have both *grades* (e.g., "major" in the army) and functional *positions* (e.g., "company commander"). Figure 7–2 shows the grade-position parallel of a typical large Japanese corporation. (Actual scales of grades and positions differ from company to company.[6]) The grades are primarily the functions of seniority, and salary scales are tied to them. Complicated formulae are used in most firms for grade promotion, according to which the more capable workers are promoted faster than the less capable ones.

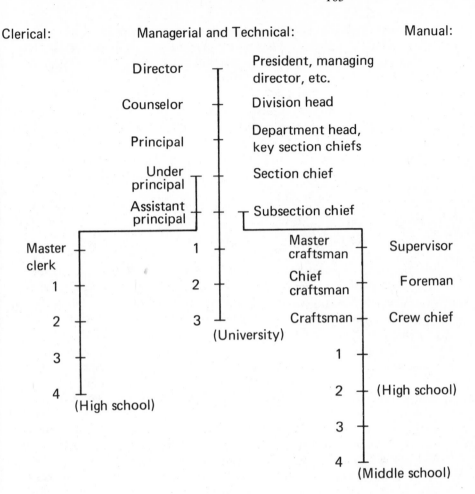

Note: *Grade* designations are to the left of the vertical lines; *position* designations are to the right.

Figure 7–2. Typical Rank Gradation in a Large Japanese Corporation.

Managerial and technical workers reach the grade of assistant principal in about ten to fifteen years after entering the firm. At the managerial level, there is a fairly close correspondence between grades and positions. Thus, most under principals, for example, may hold positions of section chief, while principals may be department heads and some key section chiefs, and so on. Clerical workers also rise through the grades, but there are few position designations in this category of workers. The most capable of them may be promoted to the position of subsection chief in the largest of Japanese firms, while in lesser firms some may reach the position of section chief within a few years of their retirement. At the blue collar level, the grade/position correspondence is not very close. Although grade promotion continues as the workers gain in seniority and skill, supervisory positions are awarded only to those with higher grades who are skillful in interpersonal relations. Higher grades, in other words, are a necessary but not sufficient condition for higher positions. Consequently, although most supervisors have high grades, not all workers with high grades are supervisors. Older workers who have high work skills but are poor in human relations are kept out of supervisory positions; they have at least high grades and the attendant high status and wages.

Semipermanent Employees

Female white and blue collar workers are not considered as permanent members of the corporate community since they are expected to leave, and most of them do leave, the firm at marriage or at first pregnancy. Some firms used to have discriminatory retirement rules for women (e.g., retirement at age thirty), but in recent years courts have ruled against these retirement rules as unconstitutional. The discrimination against women is deeply rooted in Japan's cultural traditions. Women's natural place is said to be in the home. Most female workers themselves consider their jobs as transient—as opportunities to see the outside world between their schooling and marriage. Partly because of this attitude but partly reinforcing it, firms do not treat women seriously. Large corporations as well as government offices take few women as managerial employees. In a typical Japanese corporate or government office, one-half to two-thirds of the staff members are male managers, and the rest are clerical workers, mostly women. These female employees do mostly routine clerical work, including endless serving of tea to male workers and visitors. In general, women work without concern for promotion. Even in production jobs, women are given simple unskilled works because the company knows that most women quit their jobs after several years of service. When a female employee leaves the firm, her regular-employee status is lost. The tenure, once broken, cannot be reinstated. If she wishes to return to the same company later in her life, she can do so only as a temporary worker.

This is not to say that professional careers are closed to women. Increasingly larger numbers of college (mostly junior college) educated women are moving into the corporate world, especially in the media, advertising, entertainment, and services. To find out the attitude of women office workers, *Nikkei Business* conducted in December 1975 an attitude survey of 980 college-educated female office workers in 25 large business corporations. The summary responses of the 685 who returned the questionnaire are as follows: (1) Only about one-third (34 percent) of the respondents are satisfied with their jobs; (2) 76 percent of the women plan to quit their jobs at marriage or at first pregnancy, but 20 percent want to continue to work; and (3) only 3 percent of the women believe that there is no difference in abilities and aptitudes between men and women.[7]

Temporary Workers

Firms find the use of temporary workers convenient, since they can be hired at wages markedly lower than those of regular workers and can be easily dismissed when their (usually short-term) contracts expire. They also require few fringe benefits. By resorting to the use of temporary workers, firms can weather the storms of business fluctuations while keeping the regular workers fully employed at all times.

Shortages of unskilled workers that developed in the 1960s have resulted in the reduction of the number of temporary workers employed by large corporations. In manufacturing establishments employing more than 500 workers, the percentage of temporary workers in the male work force fell from 11 percent in 1959 to 4 percent in 1970.[8] Labor shortages also prompted the firms to promote temporary workers to regular worker status. Along with the trend to promote them, the once rigid line of demarcation between the two categories has become fluid. The line is still visible in large establishments, but is rapidly disappearing in smaller firms. Most of the temporary workers today are part-time women workers and seasonal workers, largely farmers whose roots are on farms but who work in factories during the off-season months.

Outside Workers

Most large firms subcontract parts of their work to smaller firms. When the job cannot be physically moved to the subcontractors, their workers must be brought to the larger firms' premises and work alongside of the workers of the larger firms. When this happens, the workers of the subcontractors are called outside workers.

In 1971, Yawata Iron and Steel Works of Nippon Steel, Japan's largest steelmaker, employed 27,284 regular blue collar workers and 27,236 outside workers. (Temporary workers had been absorbed into the ranks of regular workers in 1959.) Additionally, there were several thousand itinerant laborers who were supplied by (illegal) labor bosses on a day-to-day basis. The company subcontracted the most hazardous and disagreeable parts of its work. In 1970, five regular workers and twenty-two outside workers lost their lives in industrial accidents at the Yawata Works. This means that nearly one in thousand outside workers died of accidents. Additionally, about one in hundred outside workers was injured in work-related accidents.[9]

Employment Practices

Lifetime Employment

The institution of lifetime employment (*shushin koyo*) for male regular workers in large Japanese corporations is a social norm, not a legally binding rule. There is a general understanding between the company and the employees that their relations are to be continuous. Whether they are managers, clerks, or production workers, they are wedded to the company for better or worse as full members of the enterprise community.

A tenured employee cannot be dismissed, unless he has committed a grave offense such as theft; incompetence is no excuse for dismissal. Discharging permanent employees would have a serious effect on employee morale and bring about labor union militancy. Workers' pressures are, however, not the only factor limiting the management's dismissal right. Most executives have a strong emotional attachment to the institution of tenured employment. They find it difficult to deny that the system has been effective in strengthening employee loyalty and generating high labor productivity. Moreover, many executives take a personal satisfaction and pride in their roles as defenders of traditional values.

Its positive effects aside, a system of continuous employment for a sizable portion of the work force is bound to interject rigidity into a company's operations. What are the ways in which Japanese firms cope with the problem of maintaining operational flexibility with a permanent work force? First of all, the management (and the union) make sure that the company does not "get stuck" with too large a permanent work force. The number of regular workers is therefore limited to a "cyclically justifiable minimum" by a mutual agreement between management and labor. Management also tries to weed out incompetents and misfits during the probationary period (lasting from three months to a year) before the new recruits become regular employees.

Second, regular workers are frequently asked to do overtime work during periods of prosperity. Since the size of the regular work force is fixed at "cyclically justifiable minimum," the size is naturally too small to produce a normal ouput level. Daily overtime of two to three hours, and overtime work on weekends are commonplace during peak-load periods. Workers seldom refuse overtime work partly because it means added income and partly because frequent refusals affect their chances of promotion. Employees in the managerial ranks must work overtime without overtime allowance, since the law exempts firms from such payments. (Many managerial employees voluntarily refrain from taking legal paid holidays off for fear that such "disloyal" behavior might adversely affect their chances of advancement.)

Third, when the volume of business declines during a cyclical downturn, management reduces the numbers of temporary and outside workers, and reduces the amount of subcontracting. Managerial employees may be dispatched to subsidiary firms on a shukko basis. Shorter work weeks may be instituted, and the pace of work may be slowed down all around the plant so that a given amount of work will keep the workers busy longer. Workers may be allowed more time than usual for work-team meetings, often to discuss cost reduction programs. If a recession deepens, as it did in the mini-depression of 1974–76, management may have to take more drastic measures in an effort to avoid dismissing regular employees. Regular workers may be "laid off," often with 50 percent or more of their regular wages, for a few days or a few weeks at a time.[b] The firm may also offer higher-than-normal severance allowances to encourage voluntary retirement. It must be really hard pressed, often on the verge of bankruptcy, to be forced to dismiss its regular employees.

Seniority-Based Promotion

A Japanese corporation is organized into a hierarchy of ranks, and young workers recruited fresh out of schools move up in the organizational hierarchy as they grow older and gain experience. This system of seniority-based promotion is called *nenko joretsu* (*nenko* means merit of years of service; *joretsu* means ranking or progression).

Since most workers in a given category are recruited at the same time and from the same age group, there is normally a close correlation between the age and the seniority of workers. This age/seniority accordance is the key factor in the nenko promotion system. In larger society, age is highly valued. If, in a firm, an older worker must work under a younger supervisor solely because the latter is more capable than the

---

[b]This practice is called "the Japanese-style layoff." In 1975, the government, under a special legislation, subsidized firms in 238 industries to the extent of one-half (two-thirds for smaller firms) of their layoff wages for six months, later extended to nine months for 188 industries. (*Asahi Shinbun*, 29 June 1975.)

former (without other justifying qualifications such as educational backgrounds), the older worker suffers a loss of face and may become resentful. Such an anomalous situation would be disruptive of group harmony and counterproductive in a rank-sensitive Japanese social organization. The nenko promotion—a ranking system based on seniority and age—helps minimize age/rank anomalies and thereby serves an important function of bringing the industrial system into line with its social milieu.

Since nenko and the performance of individual workers are never perfectly correlated, strict adherence to nenko in promoting employees introduces an element of irrationality into the firm's operations. In application, therefore, the nenko system must be flexible, and indeed it has been; several factors combine to prevent it from becoming a simple escalator. First, competence is not ignored by any means. Capable workers *are* promoted faster than others. The difference in the pace of promotion is subtle but perceptible. There is a minimum acceptable age and length of service for every position, and the less competent fall behind the minima by a progressively wider margin as they move up in the hierarchy. The more competent are promoted a year or two before the others in the same age group, and/or put in charge of more important positions or given special assignments. It is therefore easy to read the message as to who are highly regarded by the top management.

Second, as discussed earlier in the chapter, some firms have two scales of employee ranks—grades and positions. Management could therefore promote everybody in grade in step over time and pay higher wages accordingly, while putting only the more competent in charge of more important positions. This strategy might not work well for managerial ranks, however, since there is a close correspondence between managers' grades and positions.

Third, there is the bottom-up decision-making process discussed in the preceding chapter. Younger employees are encouraged to participate in decision making, and older superiors are flexible in delegating tasks and accepting the subordinates' recommendations. Consequently, the potential damage done by the incompetence of older workers who occupy higher ranks is minimized, and the capabilities of younger workers can be fully utilized. Without this flexibility, the nenko system would probably be unworkable. The more capable younger employees would not regard it as exploitation since they know that by playing the game by the rule they will advance sooner or later (and more sooner than later if they are capable).

Seniority-Based Wages

The nenko system of wages is a concomitant of lifetime employment and the nenko promotion system. If a worker is to spend all of his productive years with the company, it is not necessary, or even desirable, to pay him wages in exact proportion to his current productivity. As the worker grows in age and length of service, he acquires skills and experience, and therefore becomes more valuable to the firm and to other workers. The company must spend huge sums of money on training young workers, and this investment can be recovered only by underpaying young workers and overpaying older workers relative to their productivity. Also, from the point of view of the workers' needs, age-related wages make more sense. As they grow older, their family and social responsibilities increase, necessitating increasingly larger incomes. All these considerations combined explain why the nenko wage system—paying the workers according to their age and length of service—may not be as irrational as it appears.

Outside of government offices where wages are based strictly on seniority, the nenko wage system is seldom practiced in its pure form. Many firms attempt to reward high performance in one way or another by using complex methods of calculating wages. Such items as incentive supplement, merit supplement, job-rate allowance, and job-skill allowance are commonly used. Upon closer examination, however, we find that these factors affect the seniority-based wages very little, and that in some cases accelerate the effect of nenko payment. For example, job-rate and job-skill allowances are usually in proportion to the workers' grade and position, which are closely related to their nenko. Even a "merit" supplement may not affect the nenko wage structure much, since the average percentage merit rate for each wage grade is liable to be geared to that grade's basic salary and the variation around the average is very small. It appears that the Japanese are merely adopting the form of the Western-style, pay-by-ability wages while essentially preserving the basic nenko characteristics of their traditional wage structure. Even the semiannual "bonuses" (which may constitute up to one-third of workers' annual income) are geared closely to the basic salary.[10]

The nenko wage system is practiced primarily by larger corporations. Small firms typically pay wages more in line with the workers' present productive contribution. Assuming that workers' productivity peaks in their thirties, we can expect small firms' wages to peak in the same age bracket. In 1970, wages continued to increase up to the retirement age bracket (55 to 59) in larger manufacturing firms (1,000 employees or more), while in small firms (10–99 employees) wage rates peaked at the age bracket of 30 to 34 and declined gradually after that.[11] Similarly, in 1974, in firms employing one to four workers, the highest wage rate was received by workers in the 30 to 34 age bracket.[12]

Smaller firms pay wages in proportion to worker productivity because they do not practice lifetime employment; they find lifetime employment neither possible nor desirable. They lack the ability to exploit younger workers, as larger firms do, by paying them less than their current contribution; they simply do not possess the stability and prestige of larger corporations to attract younger workers to work at exploitative wages. Since smaller firms' needs for labor are primarily in unskilled workers, they need not invest in workers' skills. They can hire unskilled older workers at low wages in a market where supply far exceeds demand. Finally, few small firms face powerful labor unions that demand financial security for older employees. All these factors combined make small firms' wage structure relatively free of the institutional rigidities of the nenko system.

Midcareer Recruitment

In recent years there has been a marked increase in midcareer recruitment (*chuto saiyo*). Some large firms have recruited experienced personnel from other firms. Such unconventional practices have been most noticeable in technical areas where certain highly demanded skills are in short supply. Dore reports that of the total entrants into manufacturing enterprises with 1,000 or more workers in 1970, only 10 percent came from other firms with more than 1,000 employees. The figure was equivalent to 1.3 percent of all male employees of manufacturing firms with over 1,000 workers.[13] In white collar occupations, midcareer recruitment by larger firms is extremely rare even today. Those who quit a firm for one reason or another may be employed by a lesser firm and at a lower status. His pace of advance in the firm would be slower than his "in-house" colleagues. In addition to formal differentiations, he must face various forms of informal discrimination and disadvantages. He suffers from the lack of membership in the "same-year-of-entry" clique, the most important reference group in any organization. In general, he would be treated as a quasi outsider and second-class citizen for years, if not forever. The life for him in the new company, naturally, would not be an overly agreeable one.

Mandatory Retirement

Closely related to the practices of lifetime employment and nenko joretsu is the custom of mandatory retirement (*teinen-sei*). This system was initially adopted as an integral part of lifetime employment. Firms wanted to secure many years of service of skilled workers by offering them guaranteed employment and seniority-based rewards, but they also wanted to make sure that they would not be burdened with highly-paid aging employees with deteriorating productivity. Their solution was to require workers to retire at a predetermined age, with a provision that they would receive a handsome severance pay calculated on the basis of the length of their service. In 1933, about 42 percent of manufacturing establishments had mandatory retirement rules, the great majority of which set the retirement age at 50 to 55. This was reasonable considering that life expectancy of Japanese males in that year was about 46.[14]

As lifetime employment and nenko wages spread to all types of workers after World War II, firms found it imperative to institute teinen-sei as a safeguard against wage-cost rigidity. Thus, the 1970 survey of the Labor Ministry showed that 97 percent of establishments employing 1,000 or more workers had mandatory retirement rules, and 62 percent of these firms set the age at 55.[15] These requirements have caused a serious social problem. Because of the recent rapid rise in life expectancy (71.2 years for males and 76.3 years for females in 1974), workers retiring at age 55 have many more years of productive life left in them. Trade unions have naturally pressed for raising of retirement ages, but so far have not been very successful in the face of the strong resistance by employers. Many firms have worked out a compromise solution, whereby retired workers may be rehired as temporary workers and at reduced wages. Even in these cases, there is no assurance that a retiree can be rehired; the company can choose whom it wants to rehire.

The real problem of teinen-sei is not so much financial as socio-psychological.[16] Workers who have been emotionally dependent on their corporate family for over thirty years find themselves suddenly "re-jected" by it. They have been accustomed to steadily rising status as their age advanced; after retirement their status declines sharply. Many retired workers thus develop severe emotional disturbances that may be called "retirement neurosis." Younger workers who witness their seniors' plight are forced to ask themselves what "lifetime" employment really means. Such an anxiety may seriously undermine the Japanese employ-ment system; the system works only as long as it provides security and emotional fulfillment to the majority of workers.

Industrial Relations

Features of Labor Organization

In 1974, there were 67,829 labor unions in Japan with total membership of 12,462,000 workers. This represented about 34 percent of the nation's labor force.[17] Many of the unions have formed national unions by indus-try. Most of these national unions in turn belong to national federations, the largest of which is the General Council of Trade Unions of Japan, or

Sohyo. In 1974, Sohyo had 4,457,000 members, or 36 percent of total union membership. About 62 percent of the Sohyo members are public employees. The Japanese Confederation of Labor (Domei), with 2,813,000 members, accounted for 19 percent of Japan's union membership in 1974.[18] The third largest federation—the Federation of Independent Unions (Churitsu Roren)—had in 1974 1,401,000 members, which accounted for 11 percent of total union membership.[19] The activities of these federations are primarily political. Sohyo backs the Japan Socialist Party (left-wing socialists), and Domei supports the Democratic Socialist Party (moderate socialists). Churitsu Roren is politically neutral.

The locus of Japanese union activities is at the plant or enterprise level. The 67,829 unions that existed in 1974 included 37,253 unit unions organized at each plant of multiplant enterprises. The average number of members was 182 on the plant basis and 381 on the enterprise basis. Multiplant-enterprise unions had an average of 3,184 members.[20] Plant unions belonging to the same enterprise often bargain collectively with the company management. National unions and federations do not control the policies, activities or management of individual enterprise unions. Although the so-called *shunto* (spring labor offensive) is organized at the industry level, actual negotiations are carried out at the enterprise level.

Craft, industrial, or Marxist "working class" unionism is antithetic to the Japanese labor union movement. As we observed in Chapter 2, the Japanese patently lack class or profession consciousness. The sense of belonging to a profession, trade, or social "class" is inherently alien to the nation's hierarchical familism. It is with the members of the same corporate family that the Japanese identify themselves most strongly. Furthermore, the wide disparity in wages, security, and working conditions among firms makes identification with workers of other firms difficult. Workers of larger firms are naturally jealous of their privileged status and benefits, and are unwilling or reluntant to share them with employees of smaller firms.

The Enterprise Union

A Japanese enterprise union is not an entity separate from the company. Its membership exactly coincides with the status of regular worker. The great majority of unions have union-shop membership. Even where there is an open shop, regular employees automatically join the union. No distinction is made between blue and white collar workers. What matters is who a person is (i.e., an employee of what company), not what he does. Excluded from the union membership are temporary and subcontract (outside) workers and managerial personnel with the rank of section chief and above. In most companies, most of the senior managers are former union members. Consequently, there is little of the management–union standoff that is typical in a Western firm. Since the union and the company are conterminous, Japanese unions are more sensitive to the company's prosperity as reflected by its sales volume or market share than are their counterparts in other nations. In return, the management seldom makes important decisions without consulting the union leadership.

Union officers are elected from among the list of regular employees holding ranks below section chief. Management often tries to influence the outcome of elections by putting (often not very subtle) pressures on employees. Elected union officers usually keep their tenure and seniority (but without pay) in the company while devoting themselves to union activities. In the cases of managerial employees, a spell in union office for a few years is considered just another assignment within the corporate organization. Union officials may not even have to be physically separated from their colleagues in their regular work, since the company usually provides offices and other administrative facilities for the union on the company premises. A successful tenure as a union official is a recognized avenue to higher positions. Management may appreciate the union officer's leadership and problem-solving abilities, or may simply wants to "kick upstairs" the tough bargainer by promoting him to a section chief. The most promising junior managers, however, tend to shun union positions. For an overwhelming majority of union officers, the future lies unmistakably in the company and not with the national union hierarchy. Some ideologically inclined blue collar workers or noncareer government officials, however, may choose the latter as their career.

Most of enterprise unions in Japan are like dormant volcanoes. As long as the company is behaving in the best interest of its regular employees in the perception of the union's membership or leadership, the union is likely to remain cooperative or even docile. Once this perception is lost, the volcano becomes active; the union becomes militant. Let management mention the necessity to dismiss permanent employees, and the volcano erupts. Violent strikes, prolonged court battles, and bloody fights between the members of the original union and those of the company-agitated breakaway union are not uncommon consequences. This situation must be clearly distinguished from the mere appearance of militancy of most unions under normal circumstances. Annual spring "offensives" with colorful (often red) banners, ideological slogans, headbands, and snake dances are stylistic rituals good trade unionists are expected to perform. While these gestures serve a cathartic function and satisfy general expectations of the membership, negotiations of substance take place on a more private level and in a more cooperative mood.

114

Notes

1. Ronald Dore, *British Factory, Japanese Factory* (Berkeley and Los Angeles: University of California Press, 1973), p. 304.

2. There is a wealth of excellent studies written in English on the Japanese employment system and industrial relation. The most useful are: Kazuo Okochi, Bernard Karsh, and Solomon B. Levine, eds., *Workers and Employers in Japan: The Japanese Employment Relations System* (Tokyo: University of Tokyo Press, 1973); Walter Galenson, "The Japanese Labor Market," in Hugh Patrick and Henry Rosovsky, eds., *Asia's New Giant* (Washington, D.C.: The Brookings Institution, 1976), chap. 9; Taishiro Shirai, "Decision-Making in Japanese Labor Unions," in Ezra Vogel, *Modern Japanese Organization and Decision-Making* (Berkeley and Los Angeles: University of California Press, 1975), pp. 167–184; Robert M. Marsh and Hiroshi Mannari, *Modernization and the Japanese Factory* (Princeton, N.J.: Princeton University Press, 1976); Ronald Dore, *British Factory, Japanese Factory* (Berkeley and Los Angeles: University of California Press, 1973); Robert E. Cole, *Japanese Blue Collar: The Changing Tradition* (Berkeley and Los Angeles: University of California Press, 1971); and Thomas P. Rohlen, *For Harmony and Strength* (Berkeley and Los Angeles: University of California Press, 1974).

3. Dore, *British Factory,* pp. 272–274.

4. Yoshino presents an excellent discussion of the historical developments of industrial paternalism and lifetime employment of production workers in M. Y. Yoshino, *Japan's Managerial System* (Cambridge, Mass.: The MIT Press, 1968), pp. 65–84.

5. Dore, *British Factory,* p. 275.

6. For example, see Dore, *British Factory,* chaps. 2 and 3; and Marsh and Mannari, *Modernization and the Japanese Factory,* chaps. 3, 4, 6, and 7.

7. *Japan Economic Journal,* 24 February 1976.

8. Dore, *British Factory,* p. 308.

9. Satoshi Kamata, "Rodo Geshuku no Kiroku," *Chuo Koron Keiei Mondai,* Summer 1971, pp. 312–323.

10. For a detailed description of the wage structure of Hitachi, see Dore, *British Factory,* pp. 98–110. Also see Marsh and Mannari, *Modernization and the Japanese Factory,* chap. 6 for additional examples.

11. Hisao Kanamori and Yutaka Kosai, *Nippon Keizai Tokuhon* [A reader on the Japanese economy] (Tokyo: Toyo Keizai Shinpo-sha, 1973), p. 183.

12. Ministry of Labor, *Rodo Hakusho, showa 50-nen ban* [Labor white paper, 1975] (Tokyo: Ministry of Finance, Printing Bureau, 1975), p. 264.

13. Dore, *British Factory,* pp. 307–308.

14. Kenichiro Otsubo, *Teinen-sei no Hanashi* [The mandatory retirement system] (Tokyo: Nihon Keizai Shinbun-sha, 1974), pp. 36 and 69.

15. Ibid., pp. 40 and 45.

16. Seizo Okada and Shunsuke Tsurumi, "Teinen towa Nanika," *Bungei Shunju,* September 1975, pp. 268–275.

17. Ministry of Labor, *Rodo Hakusho, showa 50-nen ban,* p. 298.

18. *Japan Almanac 1975* (Tokyo: The Mainichi Newspapers, 1975), p. 125.

19. Ministry of Labor, *Rodo Hakusho, showa 50-nen ban,* p. 301.

20. Ibid. p. 298.

8

Industrial Organization and Industrial Policy

The major traits of Japanese society discussed in Chapter 2—the familial hierarchy orientation, groupism, insider–outsider syndrome, rank and rating consciousness—are equally manifest in intercorporate relations as in interpersonal relations. In a country where both enterprises and the entire nation are organized on a family principle, it is unlikely that the nation's industry is organized on a totally different principle. Just as individuals feel a need to belong to a group and draw emotional satisfaction from it, so do social organizations such as business firms. Corporations within a group are often aligned vertically, and mutual dependency and reciprocity characterize the interfirm relation. Interfirm and intergroup status competition is often fierce.

The purposes of this chapter are to examine the pattern of Japan's industrial organization, assess public policy toward industrial structure, and briefly comment on the character and activities of the big business leadership.

The Structure of Japanese Industry

The Prewar Pattern—Zaibatsu

The modern industrial sector of the Japanese economy before the end of World War II was characterized by a high degree of concentration of ownership and control under the *zaibatsu,* the large family-owned and controlled industrial and banking combines. Mitsui, Mitsubishi, Sumitomo, and Yasuda were the big four of the zaibatsu. Mitsui and Sumitomo were key merchant houses of the Tokugawa period. Mitsubishi and Yasuda began their development during the Meiji period. At the end of World War II, a quarter of the total paid-in capital of all Japanese business corporations was controlled by the big four. They and the six other lesser zaibatsu controlled one-third of incorporated business in the nation.

Each zaibatsu was a conglomerate of corporations in manufacturing, mining, trading, and finance. Few zaibatsu corporations were monopolists in their respective markets. The prevailing pattern was oligopoly. The share of the largest zaibatsu firm in a given market seldom exceeded 20 percent. What was unique with the zaibatsu industrial organization was that each combine sought to achieve an oligopolistic position in a wide range of industrial activities. In each industry, rival zaibatsu oligopolies competed for larger market shares. Cartels and other collusive actions were commonplace. Within a combine, however, firms were related to each other in a complex network of complementality and reciprocity; there seldom existed a competitive relation among the firms in the same zaibatsu group.

A typical zaibatsu consisted of several key subsidiaries, which were themselves large manufacturing, mining, trading, or financial concerns. These core companies were controlled by a holding company (*honsha,* or the main company) which was closely owned by the zaibatsu family.[a]

The pyramid-like control was extended downward by means of the following set of devices. First, the top holding company held substantial portions of the stock of the key subsidiaries, which in turn controlled second-line subsidiaries through fractional shareholding. Additionally, the family directly held blocks of stocks in the subsidiaries. There was also intercorporate shareholding among the subsidiaries. Second, the officers of the top holding company were handpicked loyal servants of the family, and the top holding company directly controlled personnel appointments of all the key subsidiaries. Third, the top holding company exercised control over subsidiaries through provision of credit. The affiliated firms held deposits in the combine bank and borrowed funds from it. This practice enhanced the holding company's control over the subsidiaries. Fourth, buying and selling were done on an intracombine basis. The group's trading company served as the sole agent for the combine, buying inputs required by member firms and selling their products to outsiders. Fifth, the *honsha* control was reinforced by interlocking directorates. One or two top officers of the core holding company held key positions in as many as fifteen subsidiaries.[1]

A zaibatsu was a family-like community not only because it was owned and controlled by a family, but also because its entire organization was based on familial principles of hierarchy, loyalty, and dependency. Institutionally, a zaibatsu combine—say, the Mitsui Zaibatsu—was not much different from the House of Mitsui of the Tokugawa period. The technology and the form of business used by the zaibatsu were modern, but the substance of the interpersonal and interfirm relations was essentially that of the hierarchical familism of traditional Japan.[2]

The zaibatsu combines were predominant in the modern, capital-intensive and technology-oriented sector of the economy. The shortage of capital and the requirements of modern technology made it imperative

---

[a]The Nissan Zaibatsu, one of the lesser six, was an exception; its holding company was under no family control.

that the available capital be used in a highly concentrated manner, and indeed it was so used in large corporations under zaibatsu control. Surplus labor that could not be absorbed by the available capital was employed in the traditional sector of the economy consisting of a large number of family-operated small firms and workshops. Although this dichotomy of large and small firms is often referred to as industrial dualism, a clear-cut duality of large and small firms was not visible; the size progression from very small to very large was smooth and continuous, Moreover, firms of different sizes were linked with each other in a complex network of buyer–seller, lender–borrower relations. Larger firms with greater resources inevitably assumed a superior, oyabun-like relation to smaller and less powerful enterprises. Zaibatsu controls of smaller firms were exercised primarily through buying and selling activities of the zaibatsu trading firms and through extension of credit by zaibatsu banks. The industrial organization of the Japanese economy in the prewar days can be summarized as consisting of a family-like hierarchy of business firms of varying size with huge zaibatsu corporations at the top and one-family workshops at the bottom.

The Dissolution of Zaibatsu

In accordance with the policy of the Allied occupation authorities, the Japanese government formed the Holding Company Liquidation Commission (HCLC) in August 1946. Under the close supervision of the occupation authorities, the commission carried out the dissolution of the zaibatsu structure. Eighty-three firms were designated as holding companies by the commission. By the end of 1947, forty-two companies were dissolved. Sixteen firms went out of existence, and twenty-six other firms formed "heir" companies, often splitting into several smaller firms. The remaining forty-one firms were allowed to remain in existence after ridding themselves of holding-company characteristics.[3]

The securities and stocks of the holding companies as well as the shares which the fifty-six zaibatsu family members had held in holding companies were transferred to the HCLC. Nonzaibatsu owners of the securities and stocks were compensated for in cash, while the zaibatsu families received, as compensations, nonnegotiable, noninterest-bearing government bonds of ten year maturity. Because of the rapid postwar inflation, however, the real value of the bonds depreciated to about 5 percent of the original value of the stocks.[4] The effect of the zaibatsu family stock liquidation and the devaluation of zaibatsu assets was drastic. Not a single member of former zaibatsu families occupies a position of importance in the postwar Japanese business world.

The HCLC sold the zaibatsu stocks and securities to the employees of the liquidated companies, to security dealers, and to the general public. One consequence of the zaibatsu dissolution therefore was the diffusion of stockholding among the public. The stocks that were released by the HCLC constituted more than 50 percent of total corporate capital in the country.[5] Between 1946 and 1950, the number of stockholders in the country increased from 1.7 million to 4.3 million,[6] a development that undoubtedly contributed to the separation of ownership and control in postwar Japanese corporations.

Banks and insurance companies were virtually untouched by the HCLC, although their use of zaibatsu names were prohibited. Some 1,500 senior executives of zaibatsu firms were barred from public and corporate offices. The purge put many young men of middle ranks overnight into top management positions. The effects of all these measures were dramatic and pervasive. The ownership and control of zaibatsu families were eliminated, corporations became independent of zaibatsu groupings, younger managers were thrust into positions of power, and the ownership of the country's largest corporations became widely diffuse.[7]

Postwar Groupings—Keiretsu

After the Allied occupation ended in 1952, the Japanese government quickly rescinded the prohibition on the use of old zaibatsu trademarks and relaxed the restrictions on regrouping of former zaibatsu firms. Thereupon many former zaibatsu companies began reassembling themselves under their old zaibatsu names. The new Mitsubishi Trading Company was formed in 1954 out of the host of splinter firms. In 1959, the three former Mitsui Bussan firms regrouped into a new Mitsui Bussan (Mitsui & Co.). The three former Mitsubishi Heavy Industries firms were permitted to merge into a new Mitsubishi Heavy Industries in 1963. Today, the Mitsui, Mitsubishi, and Sumitomo groups of firms once again constitute a major force in the Japanese economy. These former-zaibatsu groupings and the several other more recent groupings formed around major banks are commonly referred to as *keiretsu* (grouping; literally, alignment or affiliation).[8]

Coordination within each keiretsu is effected by periodic meetings of its presidents' club. The chief executives of the twenty-three major Mitsui firms form the Nimokukai (the Second Thursday Club) and meet on the second Thursday of every month. The twenty-seven Mitsubishi firms have the Kinyokai (the Friday Club), while the presidents of the sixteen Sumitomo firms meet under the name of Hakusuikai (the White Water Club). The purposes of these presidents' clubs are primarily coordination, consultation, and exchange of information; they by no means serve as command centers of the grouping.

There is a considerable amount of intragroup buying and selling, with the group's general trading company serving as the middleman. The group's bank and trust and insurance companies also hold shares in the member firms, but the extent of mutual shareholding is considerably less than during the prewar period. In most cases, a group bank's shareholding of a fraternal nonfinancial firm does not even reach the legal maximum of 10 percent. Typically, somewhere between 10 and 40 percent of the shares of a firm in a group are owned by others in the group. In some cases, cross-ownership is as high as 80 percent.[9] There is also an extensive interlocking of directorships, but not to the extent of allowing control of one firm by another. Member firms rely on the group bank for their financing, but here again concentration is rare.

Although there are many similarities between the prewar zaibatsu structure and the postwar zaibatsu-based groupings, there is one unmistakable difference: the postwar structure lacks a command center. There is no top holding company; there is no intragroup control by one firm or family. What exists in a former-zaibatsu keiretsu is a confederation of firms sharing the same tradition, cooperating in buying, selling, and financing (but not to the exclusion of other firms), with some cross-ties between them in the form of mutual shareholding, interlocking directors, and a coordinating committee.

In part stimulated by the regrouping of former zaibatsu firms, other major banks and industrial and trading firms began forming their own groups starting in the mid-1950s. Prominent in this development are the three groups clustering around the three major banks: Fuji, Sanwa, and Dai-ichi Kangyo. These groups are known as "banking keiretsu" as contrasted to the former-zaibatsu keiretsu. In general, there is considerably less structure and coordination in the banking keiretsu than in the former-zaibatsu keiretsu. The banking keiretsu, however, do have coordination through presidents' clubs, interlocking directors, intragroup buying and selling through the groups' trading companies, and intragroup shareholding and financing. In addition to the three banking groups mentioned above, there are other, looser alignments of firms developing around other larger banks, notably the Industrial Bank of Japan and the Long-term Credit Bank of Japan.

The membership of the six largest keiretsu (three former zaibatsu and three new banking) are summarized below. The four firms listed for each group are: the group bank, the group general trading company, and the two largest nonfinancial member firms. The numbers in the parentheses represent total 1975 deposits for the banks, total 1975 turnover for the trading firms, and 1975 capitalization for the nonfinancial firms.[10]

1. Mitsubishi Keiretsu (27 firms)
   The Mitsubishi Bank ($34,197 million)

Mitsubishi Corporation ($29,738 million)
Mitsubishi Heavy Industries ($354 million)
Mitsubishi Electric ($196 million)
2. Mitsui Keiretsu (23 firms)
The Mitsui Bank ($24,383 million)
Mitsui & Co. ($27,484 million)
Tokyo Shibaura Electric ($325 million)
Toray Industries ($163 million)
3. Sumitomo Keiretsu (16 firms)
The Sumitomo Bank ($35,432 million)
Sumitomo Shoji ($15,573 million)
Sumitomo Metal Industries ($277 million)
Sumitomo Chemical ($152 million)
4. Fuji Banking Keiretsu (29 firms)
The Fuji Bank ($36,387 million)
Marubeni Corporation ($17,492 million)
Hitachi, Ltd. ($425 million)
Nippon Kokan ($340 million)
5. Sanwa Banking Keiretsu (36 firms)
The Sanwa Bank ($32,134 million)
Nissho–Iwai ($12,779 million)
Hitachi, Ltd. ($425 million)
Kobe Steel Works ($254 million)
6. Dai-ichi Kangyo Banking Keiretsu (57 firms)
The Dai-ichi Kangyo Bank ($41,808 million)
C. Itoh & Co. ($16,539 million)
Kawasaki Steel ($298 million)
Nippon Express ($159 million)

Table 8–1 shows the relationship between the Fuji Bank (the former Yasuda Bank) and ten of the larger nonfinancial firms which belong to the Fuji banking keiretsu. The former Yasuda zaibatsu was largely a financial combine and lacked an industrial base. In recent decades, the Fuji Bank and the three Yasuda financial firms (Trust Bank, Life Insurance, and Fire and Marine Insurance) have built up a substantial keiretsu complex of industrial and trading firms that compare favorably with any one of the former-zaibatsu groups. Table 8–1 clearly indicates that neither the bank's shareholding nor its lending is significant enough to give it a lever of control over any of these firms. In the case of Hitachi, the bank is only the sixth largest shareholder and the fourth largest lender. Note also that Hitachi has not accepted an officer from the bank. These facts reveal the power relation between Hitachi and the Fuji Bank. Hitachi is such a prominent firm that the Fuji banking group is delighted to have it in its

Table 8–1
The Fuji Bank and Its Relations to Selected Group Firms

Companies	Stocks owned by Bank (%)	Bank's rank in stock-holding	Loans by Bank (%)	Bank's rank in loans	Number of officers from Bank
Hitachi (electric machinery)	2.0%	6	10.1%	4	0
Nippon Kokan (steel)	4.4	1	12.1	1	1
Nissan Motor	6.0	2	14.2	1	1
Showa Denko (chemicals)	6.8	2	9.3	2	0
Taisei Construction	5.3	2	21.3	1	0
Keihin Express Railway	6.6	2	9.3	2	1
Canon (camera)	7.7	2	20.5	1	0
Sapporo Breweries	3.2	3	9.8	2	1
Sanyo–Kokusaku Pulp	3.7	4	10.9	2	1
Marubeni (trading)	7.9	1	12.5	1	1

Source: Toshiaki Kaminogo, "Ginko o Kiru," *Bungei Shunju*, March 1976, pp. 100–101.

industrial family, notwithstanding the firm's rather weak shareholding and financing ties with the bank. Note, too, that Hitachi also belongs to the Sanwa banking keiretsu.

Some of the largest corporations, Hitachi included, have widely dispersed borrowing from banks belonging to different keiretsu. This lack of concentration is no doubt partially motivated by their concern over losing management autonomy. Another important reason is that their funding needs are so huge that no single bank can supply a predominant portion of them. Some of these large corporations—notably Nippon Steel, Nissan Motor, and Matsushita Electric—have also shifted their "primary" borrowing sources to the Long-term Credit Bank and the Industrial Bank of Japan. The keiretsu grouping of these banks is looser than that of the other banks listed above.

What motivated the keiretsu firms to group themselves? Caves failed to find evidence that group firms were more profitable than large independent companies.[11] Eleanor Hadley found that neither control through lending by the group bank nor control through trading companies was strong enough to explain the formation of the grouping. Typically, the member firms borrow from many banks, and the borrowing from the "primary" bank (i.e., the group bank) is not appreciably larger than the next largest loan.[12] Similarly, the group trading company's share of marketing for core manufacturing companies may not be much larger than that of nongroup trading firms. Many key manufacturing firms also do much selling on their own. The only advantages which the group trading firm has over its competitors are the advantage of having joint trade names and trademarks and, in some cases, the existence of directorship interlocks between the trading and the core manufacturing firms.[13] In sum, neither profitability nor common financing or trading activities explain the grouping of firms along the keiretsu lineage.

The basic motivation for the grouping of keiretsu firms lies in sociological factors. The tendency to form a group is an inherent part of Japan's cultural tradition. Just as individuals find emotional support and protection within a vertically aligned group, so do firms seek the security of group membership. In the cases of former zaibatsu firms, the emotive framework for regrouping was readily available. Loyalty to the old zaibatsu name and the pride it symbolized were a strong enough magnet to bring together all the firms that once belonged to the same zaibatsu group. It did not take long for nonzaibatsu firms and banks to group themselves in similar clusters. In a group-oriented society like Japan, prestige, influence, and power are derived primarily from group membership. When powerful corporate groupings develop, unorganized firms have few alternatives but to organize themselves into groups as a countervailing measure. The more important consideration, however, is the security which is accorded by group membership. The group bank finds a stable market for loans in the member firms. The industrial firms, in return, expect the group bank to rescue them in financial exigencies. For a lesser industrial firm, it is a good insurance policy to belong to a banking keiretsu, have one director or two from the keiretsu bank, have part of its stock owned by the bank, and have the bank as the primary source of capital funds. Under normal circumstances, the group bank will not let a member firm fail. For both the bank and the firms, the important consideration is to have an *insider* to whom they can turn in an adverse situation. In that way, their need to solicit assistance from indifferent or antipathetic outsiders can be minimized. In this light, keiretsu groupings can be seen as mutual-help societies of a sort for Japan's leading corporations.

Each of the enterprise groupings strives to be represented in every key industry so that each group will have oligopolistic shares in the whole gamut of industrial activities. This "one set" principle (that is, one set of everything is to be supplied by the group)[14] has two strong motives. On the one hand, the "one set" structure fosters much vertical and horizontal integration within the group, obviating the need to rely on outside sources for key inputs and facilities. On the other hand, the "one set" production accords much status and prestige to the group. If keiretsu A has oil refining, so must keiretsu B. Otherwise, B would be considered as less than complete and therefore inferior to A. Consequently, all the major groups tend to be represented in each industry, and they compete for status measured by the share of the market. The "one set" principle has resulted in much duplication of capital investments and what has come to be known as "excessive competition" (*kato kyoso*) in the postwar Japanese economy.

Enterprise Keiretsu

We have thus far identified two types of industrial grouping in the postwar Japanese economy: the former-zaibatsu keiretsu and the new banking (or financial) keiretsu. A third type of industrial grouping can now be examined. This is a complex of subsidiaries and subcontracting firms that surrounds a large nonfinancial corporation. A 1965 study by the Fair Trade Commission found that the top 100 nonfinancial corporations had 4,207 subsidiaries. Matsushita Electric headed the list with 285 subsidiaries; an average parent company had 42 subsidiaries. For this study, the FTC defined a subsidiary as a firm with parent-company shareholding of 30 percent or above, or a firm with 10 to 29 percent shareholding accompanied by interlocking directorship and/or loans from the parent firm. Of the 4,207 subsidiaries thus defined, 82 percent had parent-firm shareholding of 30 percent and above, 76 percent had parent-company management interlocks, and 37 percent had loans from the parent company.[15]

This type of industrial grouping has been variously called *sangyo* (industrial), *kigyo* (enterprise), or *shihon* (capital) keiretsu. In what follows, we shall refer to the cluster of subsidiaries and wholly dependent subcontractors that surround a major industrial or commercial concern as its "enterprise keiretsu."[16]

Subsidiaries are commonly referred to as *ko-gaisha* (child company) in relation to its *oya-gaisha* (parent company). The use of the words "parent" and "child" suggests the existence of a familial relationship of control and dependency. The subsidiary normally supplies parts and components to the parent company, or provides specific services. In addition to its heavy reliance on the parent firm's business, the child company is dependent on the parent for technical, managerial, and financial assistance. The parent firm exercises control over the subsidiary through this dependency relationship.

The top executives of a subsidiary may be the officers of the parent company. Subsidiaries are also places where the parent company find second-career jobs for its retired managerial personnel. Similarly, surplus or less competent employees of the parent company who cannot be dismissed because of tenured commitment may be transferred permanently to a subsidiary. The relationship between parent and child companies is therefore not merely commercial; it involves hierarchical personal relations.

A major firm normally has, in addition to its subsidiaries, an extensive list of subcontractors. These firms, as do subsidiaries, manufacture components for the major firm, or provide marketing or other auxiliary functions such as maintenance and janitorial services.

There are several cogent economic reasons for the widespread use of subsidiaries and subcontractors. One important reason is the disparity in wage rates between large and small firms. The parent company can take advantage of the low wages paid by the dependent firms when it transfers to them the labor-intensive parts of its production process. This enables the large firm to concentrate its productive activities on final assembly operations or on capital and technology-intensive aspects. Subcontracting also provides an effective cushion against fluctuations in business conditions. When the demand for the major firm's products slackens, it can maintain a high level of employment of its regular workers by reducing the amount of work fanned out to subcontractors and subsidiaries. Subcontractors also serve as a financial buffer for the larger firm. Payments to subcontractors are customarily made about half in cash and the other half in commercial bills of 90 or 120-day (sometimes 150-day) maturity. During periods of monetary tightness, the major firm may arbitrarily extend the maturity of its bills, thereby increasing the financial burden of the subcontractors. This process is known as *shiwayose* (squeezing). Larger subcontractors may squeeze their own subcontractors. The domino effect of squeezing is thus extended downward, causing inevitable bankruptcies among the smallest and the most vulnerable firms at the bottom of the pyramid.

In 1971, 355,000 (59 percent) of the 605,000 small and medium-size[b] manufacturing firms were classified as subcontractors. In machinery and textile industries, over three-quarters of smaller firms were so classified. Payments to subcontractors represented one-quarter to one-third of the values of total output of parent companies.[17] A 1974 study by the Small and Medium Enterprises Agency showed that the terms of contract were determined in the following manner. In 9 percent of the cases, the parent firm unilaterally determined the terms. In 40 percent of the cases, the terms were determined by the parent firm on the basis of the cost estimates submitted by the subcontractor. The terms were determined by mutual agreement in 46 percent of the cases. The remaining 5 percent involved competitive bidding (4 percent) and "others."[18] The same study revealed that 21 percent of subcontractors wanted to increase the degree of their dependency on the parent company (including becoming its subsidiary), 60 percent wanted to reduce their dependency, and 18 percent were satisfied with the existing relationship. The reasons given by the first group of firms for wanting to increase the degree of dependency were as follows: greater stability of the volume of business (55 percent), greater stability of both profits and the volume of business (31 percent), increased information and guidance from the parent company on managerial and technical matters (9 percent), and others (6 percent). Those who wanted to decrease dependency gave the following reasons: unstable business and small profit margins (47 percent), stable business but small profits (19 percent), desire for managerial independence (20 percent), pride in their unique skills and technology (10 percent), and others (4 percent).[19]

The General Trading Company

Each industrial keiretsu (either former zaibatsu or banking) has a bank and a general trading company at the top and a host of smaller firms at the

---

[b]Small and medium-size enterprises in manufacturing are defined as corporations with capitalization of less than 100 million yen ($333 thousand) or with fewer than 300 employees, and individual businesses with fewer than 300 employees.

bottom of the pyramid. The vertical links are provided by the enterprise keiretsu relations of the group's major concerns. The bank serves an important integrative function as the main source of capital resources. The trading company plays an equally important role of integrating the group through its diverse activities.

The general trading company (*sogo shosha*) is a uniquely Japanese phenomenon. There are some 6,000 "trading firms" (defined as wholesalers and retailers engaging in international trade), but only the largest of them, usually the top ten, are called *general* (*sogo*) trading companies. *Sogo* literally means "comprehensive." The original meaning of *sogo shosha* was "a firm that handled a comprehensive list of merchandise." Now, however, *sogo* is understood to mean primarily the wide range and diversity of their functions.

In 1974, the ten largest general trading companies handled $156 billion worth of merchandise, which was equivalent to about 38 percent of Japan's gross national product of that year and was almost twice as large as the national budget. Domestic sales amounted to $76.5 billion (49 percent of total sales), exports were $30.0 billion (19 percent), imports were $35.5 billion (23 percent), and the third-country trade amounted to $14.3 billion (9 percent). These firms handled about 55 percent of the nation's total exports and 57 percent of imports.[20]

The ten largest general trading companies are listed below with their sales for the year ending March 31, 1975, along with their banking keiretsu affiliations.[21]

Mitsubishi Corporation	$31.4 billion	Mitsubishi
Mitsui & Co.	28.8	Mitsui
Marubeni Corporation	18.5	Fuji
C. Itho & Co.	17.4	Sumitomo and Dai-ichi Kangyo
Sumitomo Shoji	17.1	Sumitomo
Nissho-Iwai Co.	13.4	Sanwa and Dai-ichi Kangyo
Tomen	8.1	Mitsui and Tokai
Kanematsu-Gosho	7.7	Dai-ichi Kangyo
Ataka & Co.	7.0	Sumitomo
Nichimen	6.9	Sanwa

It may be noted that, except for the former-zaibatsu groups, the relationship between a group's bank and the general trading firm is rather fluid. Recently the banks, including the former-zaibatsu banks, have been making increasingly larger loans to nonaffiliate trading firms.[c]

---

[c]The tie-up between C. Itoh and Ataka, which is expected to result in a merger in 1977, would place the new company ahead of the third-ranking Marubeni.

These firms handle almost anything under the sun—"from instant snack noodles to missiles." The number of individual items handled by Mitsubishi or Mitsui exceeds 10,000. The largest of these firms (Mitsui) has about 11,000 employees, while each of the smallest four typically has about 4,000 employees. The top ten trading houses have among them over 900 overseas offices, with a total of nearly 6,000 Japanese staff members and 16,000 local employees.[22] These overseas offices are linked with a most sophisticated network of computer-assisted teletype systems. A roving army of sogo shosa salesmen visit remote corners of the world, on foot if necessary, in search of new markets and new sources of raw materials for Japanese industries. They are extremely hard working people, motivated by a strong desire to increase the sales volume of their company and to contribute to the economic growth of their country. The firms send their most competent and promising employees to overseas posts, and their promotion and salary increases are less limited by seniority than in the cases of their colleagues back home and in other firms.

The primary function of the general trading companies is to handle the marketing and distribution of merchandise for commission. By the early 1960s, however, this function had come to be challenged by the propensity of big manufacturers to market their own products. Showing remarkable ability to accommodate to changing circumstances, the trading companies went through a metamorphosis from mere commission merchants to international developers and organizers of new business ventures. The following account exemplifies the comprehensive nature of the newly acquired developing and organizing functions of the general trading companies.[23]

Importation of feedstuffs had long been one of the major items handled by general trading companies. In order to increase the consumption of imported feedstuffs, Mitsui & Co. in the mid-1950s began guaranteeing chicken farmers purchases of chickens raised with Mitsui-imported feedstuffs. At first Mitsui sold these chickens to domestic chicken wholesalers, causing depressed market prices of chickens. In order to strengthen its control over the distribution of chickens, Mitsui in 1959 formed a cold storage firm and built cold storage facilities throughout the country. It also acquired the controlling interest in a meat and fowl wholesaler and put it under the Mitsui umbrella. Frozen broilers were retailed through the chain of supermarkets that were being developed by the Mitsui group.

Once the distribution system was completed, Mitsui turned to raising its own chickens. Through a technical tie-up with an American firm, Mitsui imporrted stock broilers from the United States. Eggs were hatched in the hatcheries built around the country, and the chicks were raised by subcontractors. A new industry was thus born. In 1971, Mitsui produced 60 million broilers, which accounted for 21 percent of the national output.

Other trading firms developed similar broiler raising and marketing systems within their own keiretsu networks. Mitsubishi Corporation hit upon an idea of changing the chicken-eating habits of the Japanese so that more chickens could be sold. It established a subsidiary in joint venture with an American fast food chain. Soon there were fried chicken outlets throughout the country. The story does not end here. The increased volume of chicken raising in Japan necessitated sharp increases in the importation of feedstuffs. In the late 1960s, the trading firms began developing farms in many parts of the world under joint venture arrangements for the specific purpose of growing feedstuffs.

We can see from the foregoing account that Japan's general trading companies are much more than mere commission merchants. They develop new industries and organize new business ventures both domestically and internationally. Their well-developed worldwide contacts and information networks enable them to provide a vital link to the world economy for the Japanese producers and consumers alike who tend to be isolated from the rest of the world because of the cultural and linguistic barriers.

Another important function served by the general trading companies is provision of credit to customers, particularly small businesses. Using their close ties with major banks, the trading firms borrow large amounts of low-interest money, which they lend to their customers. As a rule, the loans are made for the purposes of providing operating funds for the borrowers, selling raw materials on credit, financing new equipment purchases on a long-term basis, and discounting customers' commercial bills. The trading firms also purchase equity shares of their customers in order to develop keiretsu relations or rescue them from financial exigencies. While the major banks lend primarily to major corporations, trading companies do much commercial financing for smaller firms. For this reason, the large trading companies are often called "shadow banks."

A 1974 study by the Fair Trade Commission covering the financial aspects of the operations of the six largest general trading companies for the fiscal year 1972 revealed some interesting facts. The six firms on the average had an extremely low equity ratio of 3.4 percent. As of the end of March 1973, they had total borrowing from all sources amounting to $15.5 billion, of which $8.2 billion were from the city banks. The city banks' lending to the top six trading firms constituted 7 percent of the total lending of these banks. The interest rates on these loans were considerably lower than the rates charged by the banks on loans to other enterprises. Total lending by the six general trading firms amounted to $24.7 billion, of which $21.0 billion were short-term credit covering sales. Long-term loans to enterprises by the six firms amounted to $1.5 billion. They also owned stocks in 4,104 firms, 924 of which were larger firms listed on the Tokyo Stock Exchange. In 1,057 of these companies, one of the six trading firms was the largest stockholder. The combined capital of these 1,057 firms was $1.47 billion, which was about three times the combined capital of the six trading firms.[24]

The foregoing study gave rise to a serious public concern over the growing size and influence of large trading firms. This concern, coupled with the popular indignation over the revelation of gross profiteering and other shady practices by some of the leading trading companies, led to a ground swell of public demand for a tighter control over their activities. In September 1974, The Fair Trade Commission proposed a series of amendments to the Antimonopoly Law. One of the proposed measures called for limiting the cross-shareholding of a large corporation to a value equal to its capital or half of its net assets, whichever is larger. This proposal was widely believed to have been aimed at checking the cross-shareholding of general trading companies. According to the calculation made by the Nihon Keizai Shinbun, the six largest trading firms would have had to divest 70 percent of their total intercorporate shareholding as of the end of March 1974, if the Antimonopoly Law had been amended as proposed.[25] The FTC-initiated revision of the Antimonopoly Law, however, was aborted in the 1976 Diet in the face of the strong opposition by the MITI and the *zaikai*.

Public Policy toward Industry

The Antimonopoly Law

The U.S. occupation authorities imposed on the Japanese government, and the Japanese Diet enacted in 1947, a highly restrictive antimonopoly law. The law also established the Fair Trade Commission (FTC) as an agency to enforce the law. The American antitrust philosophy which had its roots in Anglo-Saxon individualism was totally alien to the cooperative business philosophy of Japan, where competition means intergroup rivalry for status and prestige. Outside the group, rivalry is fierce; inside it, *cooperation* rather than *competition* is the guiding principle. Both the laissez faire, perfectly competitive firm and the pure monopoly are manifestations of Anglo-Saxon individualism; in both cases the firm acts *alone*. Japan's social milieu is much more hospitable to groupism; "collusive rivalry" among oligopolies is the basic rule of behavior. Thus, the occupation-imposed Antimonopoly Law has never agreed fully with its environment ever since it was enacted.

The Antimonopoly Law of 1947 was considerably toned down as

soon as the occupation ended. The revison of 1953 made it more in line with the national tradition. Since then there have been several attempts at revising it; some have advocated for further relaxations, while others have argued for restoring some of the "stings" embodied in the original act. Neither side has succeeded, and the law now stands basically the same as it was revised in 1953.[26] In its interpretation, too, the law has become markedly relaxed; it has shifted from the strict "per se" philosophy (monopoly or restraint of trade per se is illegal) toward a "rule of reason" (only the *abuse* of monopoly power and the *unreasonable* restraint of trade are illegal).[27]

The law prohibits private monopolization, the formation of a holding company, and the employment of unfair business practices. Private monopolization is defined as individual or collusive action designed to exclude or control the business activities of others, thereby causing, contrary to the public interest, a substantial restraint of trade (Article 2–5). Article 9 prohibits establishment of holding companies. Six general categories of unfair business practices are listed in Article 2–7, including boycotts, price discriminations, and resale price maintenance. Restraint of trade (Article 3), trade associations (Article 8), cross-shareholding (Article 10), interlocking directorates (Article 13), and mergers (Article 15) are not illegal per se provided they do not "substantially restrain competition in any particular field of trade."

Financial companies are prohibited from holding more than 10 percent of the total outstanding shares of another company unless a prior approval of the FTC is obtained. Intent to effect a merger must be reported to the FTC thirty days in advance. The commission can disapprove the merger if it finds that the merger would cause a substantial restraint of competition. The FTC has in the past used a 30-percent-of-market rule as a criterion for disapproving of a merger; the commission would rule that a merger would cause a substantial restraint of competition if the combined market share of the merging firms exceeded 30 percent.

The Fair Trade Commission (*Kosei Torihiki Iinkai*) is a semiautonomous, quasi-judicial agency formed after the pattern of the U.S. federal agency. Although the commission is administratively attached to the Prime Minister's Office, the chairman and the four commissioners "shall exercise independent authority" (Article 28). They are appointed by the prime minister with the consent of both houses of the Diet. They serve renewable five year terms. The commission has a power to summon individuals by subpoena, conduct a search of premises, and order individuals and corporations to surrender records to it. It can hold hearings, and upon finding that the Antimonopoly Law has been violated, order the violator to cease and desist. The defendant can appeal the commission's ruling to the Tokyo High Court. The court, however, can overrule the commission's decision only when it finds that the decision is supported by faulty or insufficient evidence or it is in violation of the constitution or other laws (Article 82).

One of the most significant features of the Japanese Antimonopoly Law is the legalization of cartels formed for economic reasons. Article 24–3 permits a temporary cartel as a means to overcome hardships generated by an economic recession. The producers in a given industry can legally agree to limit the volume of production or sales, limit capacity expansion, or fix the prices. These acts are permissible when there exists an excessive supply of the commodity resulting in the price falling below the average production cost *and* the continued existence of a considerable portion of the industry is threatened. The "recession cartels" must be approved in advance by the FTC, and the membership must be voluntary.

Furthermore, Article 24–4 authorizes "rationalization cartels" that are formed for the purposes of improving technical efficiency or product quality, or of reducing costs, by means of restricting the competitive use of new technology or limiting product lines. Collective restraint on price or the volume of output is not permitted. The FTC cannot approve rationalization cartels when they (1) are injurious to the interests of the consumers and related producers, (2) are discriminatory or compulsory, or (3) result in specialized concentration of production in the hands of a few firms.

Article 22 of the Antimonopoly Law exempts special cartels formed under special laws. Unlike the recession and rationalization cartels formed under the Antimonopoly Law, cartels formed under special legislation do not require approval of the FTC. Such cartels merely require the approval of the competent minister, who must consult or notify the commission. For this reason, special-law cartels are more numerous than recession or rationalization cartels. As of the end of March 1974, there existed no recession cartel, and only nine rationalization cartels.[28] During the 1964–73 period, an average 3.2 recession cartels were in existence, with the maximum of sixteen outstanding in 1966. The number of rationalization cartels fluctuated between ten and fourteen during the same period.[29] In contrast, there were a total of 899 special-law cartels in March 1974. They were:

591 cartels formed under the Medium and Small Enterprises Organization Law
138 cartels formed under the Export and Import Trading Law
122 cartels formed under the Environment Sanitation Law
48 cartels formed under seven other statutes [30]

The overwhelming majority of these 899 cartels were formed with the approval of the Minister of International Trade and Industry.

Even more significant than the special-law cartels are the "guidance cartels" established under the leadership of the MITI. The ministry has been effectively utilizing this device to regulate the output, prices, and investment programs of various industries and firms. The usual technique is for the MITI to announce guidelines for price increases, production cutbacks, or investment targets for an industry or for major firms. These guidelines are backed up by individual consultations with the representatives of the firms and trade associations. Explicit interfirm negotiations are deliberately avoided. The FTC's reaction to this practice is one of reluctant acquiescence. The commission admits that its jurisdiction covers only collusive actions among firms. It is powerless against collusive actions promoted by a government agency. It occasionally airs its frustration by issuing stern statements, pointing out that cartelization by administrative guidance violates the spirit, if not the letters, of the Antimonopoly Law. These warnings are politely ignored by the MITI.

Industries and firms do not always fall in line behind the flag-waving MITI. The classic example of noncompliance was the Sumitomo Metal case of 1965. In view of the oversupply of steel that was then developing, the MITI suggested that the steel industry curtail the production of crude steel. Each firm was told to set its output target at 10 percent less than the actual output of the previous year. All the firms complied except Sumitomo Metal Industries, which had been aggressively expanding output to break into the group of big steel producers. The firm balked, arguing that the formula was unfair to a newcomer. Sumitomo refused to participate in the guidance cartel. The ministry retaliated by withholding Sumitomo's license for importation of coal, which was indispensable to the production of crude steel. A compromise was reached after considerable pressures were exerted on the company by many different sources. (Similar tactics were used in the 1950s against cotton spinners; the MITI cut off imports of raw cotton.)

The MITI and Industrial Policy

The traditional pattern of business behavior in Japan is cooperation among producers under the aegis of the paternalistic government, rather than atomistic competition envisaged by antitrust laws. Firms must pull themselves together to cope with difficulties, whether they arise from recessions or the "intrusion of foreign capital." And it is the responsibility of the government to protect and promote industry for the good of the country.

Embracing this probusiness ideology, the Ministry of International Trade and Industry has single-mindedly pursued the policy of encouraging and promoting industrial concentration and industry-wide cooperative efforts. In carrying out this policy, the MITI has encountered considerable oppositions from the Fair Trade Commission, which is engaged in its own development policy with a totally different philosophy—that of promoting free competition and diffusion of economic power.

In Chapter 5 we observed that the MITI, in collaboration with the Industrial Structure Council, has formulated and implemented the basic strategy of developing heavy industries in the 1960s and knowledge-intensive industries for the 1970s and beyond. Whatever the "growth industries" of the day may be, the MITI's goal has always been to channel the movement of resources into the favored industries so that they can achieve maximum development. Domestic and imported financial and technical resources have been allocated preferentially to these industries. Various forms of tax incentives and subsidies have been formuated, enacted, and provided by MITI efforts.

The growth-industry policy is but one, albeit important, aspect of the broader industrial policy of the MITI. Additionally, the ministry takes measures to promote rationalization and reorganization of industry. *Rationalization* entails improving productive technology and facilities, and managerial techniques. *Reorganization* involves greater specialization, elimination of under- or overcapacity, and optimization of the number and size of firms in each industry. Furthermore, the ministry pursues an implicit policy of *protection* of the existing industries. Ailing industries and highly fragmented small businesses have been protected by the MITI (and other agencies) with various tax, subsidy, loan, and cartelization measures.

Although the MITI utilizes a variety of policy instruments in implementing its industrial policy, its major weapons are cartels and mergers. Whether the task is one of rationalization, reorganization, or protection, the predictable MITI prescription has been to limit competition and promote bigness. These tactics naturally conflict with the goals of the FTC and the Antimonopoly Law. Consequently, prevailing over the FTC and emasculating the Antimonopoly Law has been a collateral of the MITI industrial policy. Although the FTC has a considerable support of farmers, small business, labor, and the intellectual community, it must fight a losing battle against the overwhelming power of the organized business and the powerful economic ministries.

The MITI must often induce, prod, or pressure firms and industries to take desired actions. The ministry's administrative guidance techniques play an important role here. The cliental relations, which each sector of the economy has with the industrial (vertical) bureau of the ministry and the consultative mechanisms of advisory councils and trade associations, are very useful to the MITI in carrying out its guidance activites. The ministry's mediation of public and private loans is also an important instrument of persuasion. Before the mid-1960s, the biggest stick the MITI had over industry was its authority to issue or withhold licenses for foreign exchanges needed to pay for imported materials and technology. The ministry still has several, although less important, licensing and validating authorities. It can also use, as a tool of persuasion, its authority to provide subsidies and preferential tax treatments to selected firms and industries. The influence of the MITI over business and industry wielded through the selective uses of these carrots and sticks is thus considerable. The ministry, however, cannot always have its way. Firms may balk at its suggestions if they are convinced that the proposed measure is unfair or damaging to their interest. The Sumitomo Metal case discussed earlier was a classic example of corporate recalcitrance.

Mergers and Industrial Reorganization

The MITI's utilization of the various forms of cartelization as a tool of industrial policy was briefly noted earlier. In this subsection we examine the use of mergers by the ministry as a central instrument for effecting industrial reorganization.

The basic problem of the Japanese economy, as the MITI has perceived it for over a decade now, is the excessive fragmentation and the resultant competitive weakness of the key Japanese industries in the larger world setting. Liberalization of foreign investment, which was to have been completed by the early 1970s, was thought to expose the small firms in the key industries to the threat of takeover by powerful foreign corporations. The MITI's answer to this pressing problem was to achieve greater concentration of production in fewer and larger firms. Accordingly, the ministry began aggressively promoting corporate mergers, starting in the early 1960s.

At the peak of its power and influence over industries in the early 1960s, the MITI attempted to establish a basic framework for industrial reorganization. Incorporating the results of the study undertaken by the newly established Industrial Structure Council, the ministry proposed to the Diet the Bill for the Promotion of Specific Industries. The bill called for designating strategic industries to receive special assistances, incentives, and exemptions from the Antimonopoly Law for five years for the purpose of strengthening their international competitiveness. The program was to be carried out jointly by the MITI, industrial firms, and financial institutions.[31]

The bill was defeated in the Diet in the face of strong opposition from a coalition of not only the traditional antibusiness and antigovernment groups, but also banks and the Ministry of Finance as well as a sizable segment of organized business. Yoshino explains this unexpected outcome as follows: The Ministry of Finance's opposition was in part due to the strong interministerial rivalry. The banks were not very keen about committing themselves unduly to the industrial policy of the MITI and thereby losing their autonomy in financial matters. Although the business community was basically in agreement with the goal of the bill, it was fearful that the MITI, once the plan materialized, might upset the delicate balance of power between business and government. The business leaders advocated that the initiative in the industrial reorganization program remain with the business community, and the government limit its role to that of a facilitator of change. Besides, says Yoshino, businessmen were deeply suspicious of positive government intervention, and also had been irritated by the red-tapes involved in guidance cartels and licensing negotiations as well as by the condescending attitudes of the ministerial officials.[32]

The foregoing anecdote demonstrates the nature of the relationship between the Japanese government bureaucracy and organized business—not that the business community is antigovernment or hostile to government participation in strategic programs. Rather, businessmen in Japan, as elsewhere, are instinctively fearful and suspicious of any bureaucratic initiatives that might lead to their losing freedom and independence. What business and industry want is a paternalistic and supportive government that would allow them a free hand in pursuing their own interest. This, of course, is too much to ask of the elitist Japanese bureaucrats who, notwithstanidng their generally probusiness ideology, are primarily motivated by the desire to do great things for the nation. The higher bureaucrats are naturally suspicious of businessmen's motives and unsure of the latter's ability to exercise foresight and judgment of a kind needed to steer the development of industries for the good of the nation.

Undaunted by the failure of the Bill for the Promotion of Specific Industries, the MITI continued its efforts to promote mergers by administrative guidance throughout the 1960s. In 1964, ninety-seven shipping companies were consolidated into six groupings. A five-year moratorium on interest payments to the Japan Development Bank was offered as an inducement to the industry that was less than enthusiastic at the beginning. Also in 1964, the three former Mitsubishi Heavy Industries firms merged to form a new Mitsubishi Heavy Industries. In 1965, a merger was consummated between Nissan Motor (the second largest automobile maker) and Prince Motor (the fourth largest) after much arm-twisting by the MITI.

With the approaching of the first step of liberalization of direct foreign investment scheduled to take place in 1967, the government and the business community felt an increasingly urgent need to speed up the process of industrial consolidation. The MITI thereupon sent a memorandum to the Fair Trade Commission arguing that the FTC should consider, in deliberating on merger applications, not only the relative sizes and the number of firms in the industry, but also the competition which the applicant firms face from substitute and imported products as well as from potential foreign entrants into the indstry.[33] The FTC's response was to agree to take a flexible attitude toward mergers designed for the specific purpose of strengthening the international competitiveness of Japanese industries.[34]

The FTC's ability to arrest excessive concentration of economic power faced crucial tests when plans for two extraordinary mergers were announced in 1968. The plan to merge the three largest paper companies was aborted in the face of strong opposition of the FTC. The merger, if permitted, would have created a firm controlling over 50 percent of the market share of major paper products, including 60 percent share of the newsprint market. These figures were far in excess of the 30-percent-of-market rule the FTC had established as a criterion for approving mergers.

The case of the planned merger between Japan's two largest steel producers—Yawata Iron and Steel and Fuji Iron and Steel—turned out differently. The merger would create the second largest steelmaker in the world. The combined share of the crude steel market of these firms was 36 percent, which was in excess of the FTC's 30 percent guideline. Public opinion was vehemently against this merger. The FTC at first turned down the application. From the viewpoint of the MITI, the Yawata–Fuji merger was a very special one. The two companies were former components of the broken-up Nippon Iron and Steel which had been formed in 1934 as the result of the merger of the state-owned Yawata Iron Works and five private steel companies, including the old Fuji Steel. Prior to 1934, Yawata Iron Works had been operated directly by the Ministry of Commerce and Industry, the predecessor of the present MITI. Because of this close historical tie between the MITI and Yawata–Nippon Steel, the ministry was particularly anxious to effect the proposed merger. Yawata and Fuji also had a large number of former Commerce and Industry (later MITI) officials who had "descended" on them on an amakudari basis. (The positions of board chairman, president, and executive managing director of the new company, Nippon Steel Corporation, were occupied by former MITI officials.) To MITI officials, therefore, the merger of Yawata and Fuji was tantamount to restoring the old glory of *their* steel company; from the beginning they pressed the merger case with unusual zeal and tenacity.

The merger proposal went to a formal hearing, and MITI officials appeared as witnesses in favor of the merger. On October 30, 1969, the

FTC approved the merger on the condition that the two companies do everything possible to avoid infringing upon the Antimonopoly Law. The companies also had to agree to divest themselves of their capacity to produce rail, tin plate, and pig iron for casting. The approval was considered by many as the result of the tremendous pressures exerted on the FTC by the government and the zaikai. The FTC's decision to approve the steel merger and disapprove the paper merger was in part politically motivated. To approve both would certainly invite a public furor. To reject both, on the other hand, would make the commission look highhanded and unreasonable, and would certainly infuriate Japan's powerful and deeply entrenched establishment to the extent that the survival of the FTC and possibly of the Antimonopoly Law would be endangered. The FTC therefore made a compromise of approving one and rejecting the other. The relative strengths of the economic and political power of the two industries determined the final outcome.

Industrial reorganization is a slow process even with constant prodding of the government. Many key industries have not as yet reached a stage of concentration and strength considered satisfactory by the MITI. The automobile industry, for example, still has about a dozen producers. Only Toyota Motor and Nissan Motor, with a combined share of nearly 60 percent of the market, have large enough scales of operations. Smaller firms are allowed the luxury of independence as long as they maintain profitable operations. Once their financial conditions deteriorate, however, they come under constant governmental pressures to merge with a larger firm. In 1976, the MITI reportedly made an effort to persuade Toyota or Nissan to absorb Toyo Kogyo, the financially troubled maker of Mazda cars, appealing to their sense of social responsibility and offering them a subsidy.[35]

Mergers of firms in Japan are inherently difficult for several reasons, all of which are related to the group orientation of Japanese society. The principal stumbling block is the difficulty of merging two groups of individuals with different group identification and loyalty. Persons do not easily abandon their old company ties, and therefore they tend to form cliques in the newly merged firm. The members of a lesser firm are accorded an inferior status and are generally discriminated against by the individuals belonging to the larger group. In the Nissan–Prince merger, the former employees of Prince were looked down upon by the men of Nissan and were subjected to much humiliation.[36]

Even when two (or more) firms of roughly equal status and size merge, allocation of managerial positions in the new company is a very delicate matter. If the president of one company becomes the president of the new company, the other president must become the board chairman, and so on down the hierarchy. If positions are not equally and fairly distributed, the employees of one company lose face and become demoralized. It must be remembered, too, that all these individuals join the new firm with their entourages of kobun and kohai. Intergroup rivalry, jealousy, and petty infighting are likely to continue for years or even decades after the merger. For these reasons, employees are usually lukewarm or even hostile to a merger of their companies. Managerial personnel and the labor union of the lesser company in the proposed merger may object so strongly that the plan may be aborted. Objections of the keiretsu banks, subsidiaries, subcontractors, and distributors may also be strong enough to block the merger.[d]

Business Organizations

Trade Associations

Keiretsu are essentially groupings organized on the vertical principle. Horizontal industrial organization that cuts across keiretsu affiliations is served by the trade associations representing the interests of the owners and managers of the firms in each industry. There are more than one hundred such organizations. For example, the steel industry is represented by the Japan Iron and Steel Federation, and the automobile makers have the Japan Automobile Manufacturers Association. Banks are represented by the National Federation of Bankers' Associations, and trading companies' interests are served by the Japan Foreign Trade Association.

These associations are organized ostensibly for the purposes of promoting close relations among the members, and exchanging views and information. Article 8 of the Antimonopoly Law prohibits trade associations from engaging in any acts that result in substantially restricting competition. Many activities of a trade association—including compilation and publication of industry-wide statistics on production, costs, and prices—come very close to substantially restraining competition. The trade association often proposes to the government the formation of a cartel. Established cartels invariably work through the machinery of trade associations. These associations are therefore fertile ground for collusive business practices.

---

[d]In recent years, another source of pressure for mergers has emerged. Major keiretsu banks dispatch their officers to their client firms that are in financial difficulty, and, as one of the means of recovering their investments, engineer a merger with a larger firm. The announced merger plan of the troubled Ataka & Co. with C. Itoh & Co. has been arranged by the Sumitomo Bank, the two trading firms' common keiretsu bank.

The government encourages and welcomes the formation of trade associations because they facilitate its task of regulating and assisting the industry. The tradition dates back from the prewar days, when the entire industry was organized in a corporatist pattern of tight governmental control of business activities. Today, trade organizations serve to facilitate the two-way communication between government and industry. Each industry, through its trade association, speaks with one voice in its liaison with the genkyoku bureau which has jurisdiction over it. The government obtains the information and expertise necessary for formulating and implementing its industrial policy, either directly from trade associations or indirectly through advisory councils that are heavily represented by the officers of trade associations. The leaders of trade organizations also lobby actively for their partisan interests with government bureaus, parliamentary committees, and political parties.

Federations of Business Organizations

While a trade association's primary concern is the promotion of the interest of the industry it represents, the overall interests of the business community, particularly of big business, is articulated and aggressively promoted by the four federations of business organizations. The most powerful of the four economic federations is Keidanren (Keizai Dantai Rengokai, the Federation of Economic Organizations). Its membership consists of over one hundred trade associations, several hundred major corporations, and several large public corporations. Keidanren speaks singularly for the interest of big business. The membership of Keizai Doyukai (Japan Committee for Economic Development) consists of about 1,500 progressive business executives, whose common interests and goals are to articulate new business ideologies that are consonant with the changing times. Nikkeiren (Nihon Keieisha Dantai Rengokai, the Japanese Federation of Employers' Associations) develops and executes a common labor policy for big business, and its membership is almost identical with that of Keidanren. Nissho (Nihon Shoko Kaigisho, the Japan Chamber of Commerce and Industry) represents several hundred local chambers of commerce and industry, with a total membership exceeding a third of a million enterprises in manufacturing, finance, trade, and services. Because of the composition of its membership, Nissho speaks for the interest of small business more actively than the other three organizations.

The leadership of these four federations (with considerable overlapping) constitutes a powerful pressure group known as zaikai. The word zaikai (literally, financial or economic world) is used rather loosely, and is subject to different interpretations depending on the context within which it is used. In the broadest sense, it simply means the business community. Some define zaikai as synonymous with the four business federations listed above. In its most frequent use, however, the word zaikai refers to a circle of influential business executives, numbering perhaps less than one hundred, who occupy the positions of leadership in one or more of the four economic organizations and who are intimately in touch with the centers of political power. [Some top corporate executives are not considered as *zaikai-jin* (zaikai persons) because of their lack of zaikai activities. On the other hand, some active zaikai leaders do not hold corporate positions.] Used in this sense, *zaikai* and *zaikai shunobu* (zaikai leadership; that is, the leadership of the business community) are synonymous.

The essence of zaikai activities lies in its political dimensions. Zaikai members articulate business ideologies, promote business interests, and influence public policy making by operating within the political arena. Unlike trade associations that deal mainly with the government bureaucracy, zaikai activists work on politicians, using their personal relations built around the university ties and the channels of money politics. Zaikai is the biggest and most powerful pressure group operating on the political process in Japan. No major policy steps are taken by the government without first consulting the zaikai leaders. Zaikai even has power to influence the choice of a prime minister, although it is not always successful.

The influence of zaikai on Japanese politicians derives from its role as the primary source of political contributions. Corporations, trade associations, and business federations all contribute enormous sums of money to politicians, political parties (largely the ruling conservative party, LDP) and factions within the parties. Because of the peculiarities and (convenient) imperfections in Japan's laws concerning political contributions, the bulk of political funds comes from corporate sources but remains hidden from public scrutiny. One of the key functions of Keidanren is to allocate contribution quotas to its constituencies. Conservative party (LDP) politics and election campaigns thrive on the massive flow of funds thus collected. Zaikai thus plays the strategic role of the biggest fund raiser in Japan's money politics, and its "purchase" of political influence completes the three-way, jankenpon circle of influence and power between the party government, bureaucracy, and big business.

Notes

1. Eleanor M. Hadley, *Antitrust in Japan* (Princeton, N.J.: Princeton University Press, 1970), pp. 27–29, 82–83.

2. For the role played by zaibatsu in the prewar Japanese economy, see: ibid., chaps. 1–3; and Kozo Yamamura, *Economic Policy in Postwar Japan: Growth versus Economic Democracy* (Berkeley and Los Angeles: University of California Press, 1967), chap. 7. For the historical development of zaibatsu families dating from the Tokugawa period, see Johannes Hirschmeier and Tsunehiko Yui, *The Development of Japanese Business 1600–1973* (Cambridge, Mass.: Harvard University Press, 1975), pp. 57–66, 132–142, and 212–224.

3. Yamamura, *Economic Policy in Postwar Japan*, p. 5.

4. Ibid., p. 11.

5. Hisao Kanamori and Yutaka Kosai, *Nippon Keizai Tokuhon* [A reader on the Japanese economy] (Tokyo: Toyo Keizai Shinpo-sha, 1973), p. 104.

6. Yamamura, *Economic Policy in Postwar Japan*, p. 6.

7. For further information on zaibatsu dissolution, see Hadley, *Antitrust in Japan*, chaps. 4–10.

8. For further details on keiretsu, see: ibid., chaps. 11 and 12; and Dan Fenno Henderson, *Foreign Enterprise in Japan: Laws and Policies* (Chapel Hill, N.C.: University of North Carolina Press, 1973), pp. 130–141.

9. Hadley, *Antitrust in Japan*, pp. 212–219.

10. *Japan Almanac 1975* (Tokyo: The Mainichi Newspapers, 1975), pp. 405–424. For a complete listing of the memberships of these six keiretsu, see Henderson, *Foreign Enterprise in Japan*, app. VII.

11. Richard E. Caves, "Industrial Organization," in Hugh Patrick and Henry Rosovsky, eds., *Asia's New Giant* (Washington, D.C.: The Brookings Institution, 1976), chap. 7, p. 522.

12. Hadley, *Antitrust in Japan*, p. 226.

13. Ibid., pp. 247–248.

14. Yoshikazu Miyazaki, *Sengo Nihon no Keizai Kiko* [The economic organization of postwar Japan] (Tokyo: Shinhyoron, 1966), chap. 2.

15. Hadley, *Antitrust in Japan*, pp. 291–293.

16. For further information on enterprise keiretsu, see: ibid., chap. 13; and M. Y. Yoshino, *Japan's Managerial System* (Cambridge, Mass.: The MIT Press, 1968), pp. 148–161.

17. Small and Medium Enterprises Agency, *Chusho Kigyo Hakusho, showa 50-nen ban* [White paper on small and medium enterprises, 1975] (Tokyo: Ministry of Finance, Printing Bureau, 1975), p. 238.

18. Ibid., p. 239.

19. Ibid., p. 247.

20. *Japan Almanac 1975,* pp. 98 and 469.

21. Ibid., p. 98; and *Business Community,* Autumn 1975, p. 75.

22. Nikkei Business Henshu-bu, *Nihon no Kigyo Kankyo* [The environment of Japanese business] (Tokyo: Nihon Keizai Shinbun-sha, 1974), pp. 25 and 129.

23. This account is based on Ryusuke Kikuiri, "Shosha: Nippon Gensan no Monsuta," *Bungei Shunju,* November 1972, pp. 261–262.

24. Fair Trade Commission, *Sogo Shosha ni Kansuru Chosa Hokoku* [Study Report on General Trading Companies] reprinted in *Chuo Koron,* April 1974, pp. 129–137.

25. *Industrial Review of Japan/1975* (Tokyo: The Japan Economic Journal, 1975), p. 126.

26. For further information on the postwar controversy over antitrust legislation, see: Hadley, *Antitrust in Japan,* chaps, 6, 14, and 15; Yamamura, *Economic Policy in Postwar Japan,* chaps. 4–6; and Chitoshi Yanaga, *Big Business in Japanese Politics* (New Haven, Conn.: Yale University Press, 1968), chap. 6.

27. Henderson, *Foreign Enterprise in Japan,* p. 151.

28. Fair Trade Commission, *Kosei Torihiki Iinkai Nenji Hokoku, showa 49-nen ban* [Fair Trade Commission annual report, 1974] (Tokyo: Ministry of Finance, Printing Bureau, 1974), p. 238.

29. Caves, "Industrial Organization," in Patrick and Rosovsky, eds., *Asia's New Giant,* p. 487.

30. FTC, *Nenji Hokoku, showa 49-nen ban,* p. 238.

31. Yoshino, *Japan's Managerial System,* pp. 184–185.

32. Ibid., pp. 186–187.

33. K. Bieda, *The Structure and Operations of the Japanese Economy* (Sydney: John Wiley and Sons Australasia, 1970), p. 223.

34. Yoshino, *Japan's Managerial System,* p. 192.

35. *Business Week,* 15 March 1976, p. 41.

36. Chie Nakane, *Japanese Society* (Berkeley and Los Angeles: University of California Press, 1972). p. 57.

9

Finance, Banking, and Monetary Policy

Business in a modern economy is conducted largely by means of money and credit. Consequently, institutions related to money, credit, and banking uniquely shape the character of an economic system. Although the technology of transferring financial resources is essentially the same throughout the world, financial organization and behavior patterns are subject to a considerable degree of variation from country to country, since they are affected to a large extent by historical and cultural factors. In this chapter we examine the flow of funds in the Japanese economy, the corporate debt structure, various types of financial institutions, money and capital markets, and the Bank of Japan and its monetary policy.[1]

The Flow of Funds

A study of the debtor–creditor relationships between the various sectors of a modern market economy usually shows that the personal (household) sector is a net lender and the corporate (business) sector is a net borrower. The basic pattern is that of households supplying their savings to corporations, which use the funds for productive investments. In this section, our attention will be focused on how this main flow of funds is channeled in the Japanese economy.

The Japanese save about 20 percent of their disposable income. This compares favorably with the average saving ratios of other industrialized nations (5 percent in the United Kingdom, 7 percent in the United States, and 16 percent in West Germany). This large volume of savings finds its way via various channels largely to the corporate sector. The other side of the coin of high personal saving is the heavy borrowing of corporations. The financial system facilitates this massive transfer of investible funds, thereby contributing to the high rate of capital formation in the corporate sector and the high rate of growth of the national economy.

Table 9–1 shows the intersector financial transactions, for fiscal 1973, of three selected sectors: financial institutions (exclusive of the Bank of Japan), corporate business, and personal. Although the transactions among four other transactors—the Bank of Japan, the national government, the public corporations and local authorities, and the rest of the world—must also be examined in order to see a complete picture, we can nevertheless observe in a broad outline the mainstream of funds that flow from the personal sector to the corporate sector via financial institutions. In fiscal 1973, the corporate sector's deficit of $26.7 billion was very roughly balanced by the personal sector's surplus of $31.3 billion.[a] These figures actually understate the contribution made by the households to the nation's capital formation because the "personal" sector includes noncorporate business firms which did much borrowing. The households' contribution of investible funds can be more accurately indicated by the sum of the sector's acquisition of savings deposits ($47.3 billion) and bonds and stocks ($4.9 billion).

The personal sector's savings deposits ($47.3 billion) constituted the largest source of the loanable funds made available to the financial institutions. The latter in turn loaned about the same amount ($48.7 billion) to the corporate sector. One of the unique characteristics of Japanese corporate financing emerges from this analysis. It is the extremely high reliance on bank loans and scanty uses of bonds and stocks for raising corporate capital. Compared to the $48.7 billion loans from financial institutions, the corporate sector raised only $5.6 billion in stocks ($3.4 billion) and bonds ($2.2 billion).

Of all the transaction categories listed in Table 9–1, the most important are (1) savings deposits, and (2) loans; the former identifies the sources of funds and the latter shows who borrowed how much. Focusing our attention on these two categories, and adding extra information on other sectors that is not shown in Table 9–1, we find the following result: Savings deposits totaling about $55 billion were made in financial institutions ($42 billion) and in the government's Trust Fund Account (post office savings, postal life insurance, etc., $13 billion). Combining these and other deposits with the $13 billion in loans from the Bank of Japan, the financial institutions made loans totaling approximately $67 billion. The national government sector, largely through its Trust Fund Account, loaned an additional $17 billion. The total lending of $85 billion was distributed as follows: $9 billion to public corporations and local governments, $49 billion to corporate businesses, and $27 billion to the personal sector—that is, largely to noncorporate business firms. This admittedly very sketchy way of looking at the flow of funds within the Japanese economy nevertheless shows us in a bold relief the general pattern of the Japanese financial system.

---

[a]More precisely, the surpluses of three sectors (personal, $31.3 billion; national government, $7.5 billion; rest of the world, $3.7 billion) were matched by the deficits of two sectors (public corporations and local governments, $15.9 billion; corporate business, $26.7 billion). For complete information, see the source cited for Table 9–1.

Table 9–1

Net Acquisitions of Financial Assets and Net Increases in Liabilities, Selected Sectors, Fiscal 1973

(Billions of Dollars)

Transaction Category	Private Financial Institutions		Corporate Business		Personal[b]	
	Assets	Liab.[a]	Assets	Liab.	Assets	Liab.
Currency	$0.9		$0.4		$4.0	
Demand deposits	2.7	$15.4	8.7		6.2	
Savings deposits[c]		42.3	8.2		47.3	
Bonds and stocks	8.0	7.4	2.8	$5.6	4.9	
Loans[d]	67.6	12.3[e]		48.7		$26.9
Trade Credit			87.9	84.4		3.5
Others		1.8	4.0		−0.6	
Surplus or deficit(−)				−26.7		31.3
Total	79.2	79.2	112.0	112.0	61.8	61.8

Source: Bank of Japan, Statistics Department, *Economic Statistics Annual, 1974,* pp. 17–18.
[a]Liabilities.
[b]Includes households and noncorporate business.
[c]Include time deposits, trust fund deposits, deposits in trust bank accounts, and insurance.
[d]Include call loans, commercial bills, and Bank of Japan loans.
[e]Practically all of this is loans from the Bank of Japan.

The Corporate Debt Structure

The financial structure of the corporations in all industries as of March 31, 1975, is presented in Table 9–2. Two points are noteworthy. First, the equity ratio is extremely low (14.3 percent) by the Western standards. In the United States and the United Kingdom, the ratio is typically above 50 percent. Second, within the external financing, the proportion of bond financing is very small. These two features are part and parcel of the same unique characteristic of Japanese corporate finance, namely, its heavy reliance on bank borrowing.

Before World War II, the equity ratio of all Japanese industries was over 60 percent. Since the end of the war, the ratio has decreased steadily, and, by March 1975 had reached 14.3 percent. Large external debts take a toll in the form of high debt-service costs. While the interest costs in the United States are typically about 1 percent of gross sales revenue and are much smaller than depreciation charges or net profit, for Japanese manufacturing firms they average about 5 percent of revenue and are about equal in size to the average depreciation cost or net profit.[2]

Various reasons have been offered to explain the low equity ratio of

Table 9–2
Financial Structure of Corporate Business, All Industries, End of March 1975
(Percentages)

Category	
Current liabilities	60.4%
Trade credit	28.0
Short-term loans from financial institutions	17.3
Others	15.1
Long-term liabilities	25.3
Bonds	1.7
Loans from financial institutions	17.3
Others	6.3
Equity	14.3
Total	100.0

Source: Ministry of Finance, *Zaisei Kinyu Tokei Geppo* [Monthly fiscal and financial statistics], November 1975, p. 16.

Japanese corporations. Rapid growth of the Japanese economy has been blamed for making internal accumulation of capital difficult. Another often-cited reason is that equity financing is more expensive than external financing, since interest costs are tax deductible whereas dividends are not. Wallich and Wallich convincingly argue that the most important single reason for the unpopularity of equity financing in Japan is the fact that equity financing commits the firm to deliver to stockholders a fixed proportion of a growing stream of earnings, while debt financing costs the firm a diminishing proportion of future earnings.[3]

The lopsided structure of financing makes a typical Japanese firm highly vulnerable in severe business recessions. The danger, however, is not as great as it would appear, at least for large corporations in keiretsu groupings. When a large firm is affiliated with a city bank with which it has established close personal and financial ties, the bank will simply not let the firm fail. Even then, the management of the firm must be prepared to give up part of its autonomy, since the bank would be likely to insist on placing its officer(s) in the company's management. Smaller firms and large corporations that have chosen not to be affiliated with a keiretsu bank are less fortunate. The withdrawal of loans by one bank would trigger panic withdrawals of funds by lesser lenders, which might eventually force the firm to fail. The widely publicized bankruptcies of Nihon Netsugaku in 1974 and of Kohjin in 1975 fell in this category. (Kohjin, a paper and pulp company with prebankruptcy annual sales of $270 million, was the largest company ever to fail in Japan. It had a debt of $500 million.)

The Financial Institutions

The financial system of Japan consists of a mixture of private and public institutions that vary greatly in size, purpose, and clientele. The following list presents in a summary form the whole array of these institutions. The numbers in parentheses indicate the number of institutions in each category as of the end of 1974.[4]

1. The Bank of Japan
2. Banks
    City banks (13)
    Regional banks (63)
    Trust banks (7)
    Long-term credit banks (3)
3. Financial institutions for small businesses and cooperatives
    Mutual loan and savings banks (72)
    Credit associations (476)
    Credit cooperatives (491)
    Agricultural cooperatives (5,002)
    The Shoko Chukin Bank
    The Norin Chukin Bank
    Others
4. Government financial institutions
    The Japan Development Bank
    The Export–Import Bank of Japan
    Public corporations of loan and finance (10)
5. Others
    Life insurance companies (20)
    Non-life insurance companies (22)
    Securities finance companies (3)
    Securities companies (236)

Table 9–3 shows the magnitude of the outstanding loans and discounts of these financial institutions as of the end of 1974. Loans made to other financial institutions are subtracted to eliminate double counting. The table shows that over a half of the loans and discounts have been provided by the four types of banks, and over a quarter of lending has been done by the city banks alone. The financial institutions for small businesses and cooperatives are responsible for nearly one-quarter of lending, while the government financial institutions have provided about one-tenth.

150

Table 9–3
Loans and Discounts Outstanding by Financial Institutions, End of 1974

Institutions	Loans and Discounts[a] ($ billions)	Percentage Distribution
City banks	$143.5	26.1%
Local banks	79.2	14.4
Trust banks[b]	45.4	8.3
Long-term credit banks	32.8	6.0
Mutual loan and savings banks	36.2	6.6
Credit associations	44.3	8.1
Credit cooperatives	11.4	2.1
Agricultural cooperatives	23.5	4.3
Shoko Chukin Bank	9.5	1.7
Norin Chukin Bank	5.6	1.0
Japan Development Bank	9.5	1.7
Export–Import Bank	8.9	1.6
People's Finance Corporation	5.8	1.1
Housing Loan Corporation	9.3	1.7
Agriculture, Forestry & Fishery Corp.	5.6	1.0
Small Business Finance Corporation	6.6	1.2
Six other loan & finance corporations	7.0	1.3
Life insurance companies	24.1	4.4
Non-life insurance companies	3.5	.6
Others	37.9	6.9
Total	549.6	100.0

Source: Bank of Japan, Statistics Department, *Economic Statistics Annual, 1974.*
[a]Exclusive of loans to other financial institutions.
[b]Includes trust accounts of other banks.

The Banking System

Of the four types of banks enumerated above, the first two (city banks and regional banks) are called "ordinary banks" (*futsu ginko*). This term is the closest equivalent of the English term "commercial banks."[b] The city banks (*toshi ginko*) include the following major banks, listed in the descending order of the size of their deposits as of March 1976: Dai-ichi Kangyo, Fuji, Sumitomo, Mitsubishi, Sanwa, Tokai, Taiyo-Kobe, Mitsui, Kyowa, Daiwa. Saitama, Hokkaido Takushoku, and Tokyo. These banks have head offices in large cities and, in 1974, had 2,427 branches throughout the country. The sixty-three regional banks (*chiho ginko*) had 4,549 branches in 1974. These banks are on the average much smaller than city banks, and their operations are largely limited to one prefecture.

The difference between city and regional banks is more qualitative

[b]In this book, "ordinary banks" and "commercial banks" are used interchangeably.

than quantitative. The city banks serve primarily large corporations, while the regional banks cater to other types of business. In 1974, two-thirds of the city banks' loans were to large borrowers, while six-tenths of the regional banks' loans were to small and medium enterprises. Because of the massive need for investible funds in the modern industrial sector, the city banks have been perpetually short of funds, while the regional banks have not always been able to turn their expanding deposits into loans. Consequently, the city banks have borrowed the excess funds of the regional banks and other financial institutions in the money markets. The city banks have also relied heavily on loans from the Bank of Japan (BOJ). In 1974, the city banks' borrowing of $4.8 billion from the BOJ constituted 3.4 percent of their total loans and discounts, while the comparable figure for the regional banks was 0.25 percent. Because of the city banks' perennial shortage of cash and their importance as the primary source of investible funds for large corporations, the BOJ considers them as a strategic target of its monetary policy. The city banks are closely regulated by the BOJ in exchange for their privileged access to the Bank's financial resources.

The trust banks (*shintaku ginko*) deal with the traditional trust business; that is, they manage the funds entrusted to them by trustors (individuals, institutions, pension funds, etc.). Before World War II, this business constituted the bulk of the trust banks' activities. Since 1952, however, the trust banks have issued negotiable loan-trust certificates and lent the funds thus raised to large firms as medium-term loans. Over 50 percent of their funds are now raised in this manner. Consequently, trust banking has become much akin to savings banking. In addition, all the seven trust banks now engage in regular commercial banking business. In contrast, only one ordinary bank (the Daiwa Bank) handles trust banking business. The trust bank in each keiretsu, along with its life and non-life insurance companies, serves as a powerful ally of the keiretsu city bank in group financing.

There are three long-term credit banks: the Industrial Bank of Japan (*Nippon Kogyo Ginko*), the Long-term Credit Bank of Japan (*Nippon Choki Shinyo Ginko*), and the Nippon Fudosan Bank (formerly known in English as the Hypothec Bank of Japan). These banks' lending activities are limited to equipment loans and loans for long-term working capital. The first two banks cater to large corporations, while the Nippon Fudosan Bank serves chiefly smaller enterprises. These banks are permitted by law to issue bank debentures of one- to five-year maturity in value up to twenty times their total capital and reserves. They can accept deposits only from their borrowers, and the national and local governments. In 1974, the size of their deposits was equal to about 22 percent of their outstanding debentures. As of the end of 1974, 73 percent of all bank debentures outstanding were those issued by the long-term credit banks.[c]

Commercial Banking

We saw in Table 9–3 that 40 percent of loans and discounts outstanding were held by commercial (i.e., city and regional) banks. Let us examine in some detail the nature and magnitude of the business of these banks. Table 9–4 shows the combined balance sheet of the city and regional banks as of the end of 1974.

The Asset Side. While they differ markedly in average size, the two types of banks do not exhibit a significant difference in their asset structure. In both types of banks, loans and discounts are the largest asset items, followed by securities.

Table 9–4
Combined Balance Sheet of Commercial Banks, End of 1974
(Billions of Dollars)

	City Banks	Regional Banks
Assets:		
Currency	$1.84	$1.99
Checks and bills on hand	15.15	3.20
Deposits with others	4.56	3.18
Call loans	.31	2.51
Securities	25.58	14.91
Loans	107.82	57.91
Discounts	35.67	21.31
Customers' liabilities for debt guarantees	28.67	5.75
Other assets	23.78	5.03
Total	243.38	115.78
Liabilities and net worth:		
Deposits	154.73	97.01
Loans from the Bank of Japan	4.82	.19
Call loans	7.68	.30
Bills sold	16.76	.04
Debt guarantees	28.67	5.75
Other liabilities	17.89	3.05
Capital, reserves, and surpluses	12.85	9.43
Total	243.38	115.78

Source: Bank of Japan, Statistics Department, *Economic Statistics Annual, 1974.*

---

[c]In addition to the long-term credit banks, the Bank of Tokyo (under the Foreign Exchange Bank Law), the Norin Chukin Bank, and the Shoko Chukin Bank are authorized to issue bank debentures.

Securities. The percentage distribution of the various types of securities held by commercial banks is shown below:

Government bonds	8.6 percent
Local government bonds	20.9
Corporate debentures	12.2
Bank debentures	23.4
Public corporation bonds	11.6
Stocks	17.9
Others	5.4

As for the composition of their security holdings, the two types of commercial banks show little difference except that the city banks have an appreciably higher percentage holding of corporate stocks (24 percent) as compared to the regional banks (7 percent). Close to one-third of all bank debentures outstanding are held by commercial banks. These banks purchase long-term credit banks' debentures partly as investments (particularly during periods of monetary ease), and in part as a means to facilitate their customers' obtaining loans from the long-term credit banks.

Loans and Discounts. Approximately two-thirds (68 percent) of commercial banks' loans are in the form of "loans on bills;" that is, loans made by the banks discounting negotiable promissory notes issued by the borrowers in the banks' favor. This type of loan is used primarily for financing working capital of the borrower, and therefore the terms of notes seldom exceed three months. In many cases, however, the notes are renewed upon maturity, so that they are de facto long-term loans. About a third (31 percent) of commercial bank loans are "loans on deeds." The borrower gives the bank a bond of debt (a nonnegotiable promissory note) secured by real estate as a collateral. These loans are used primarily for financing purchases of plant and equipment. The remaining 1 percent of commercial bank loans is overdrafts on current accounts.

Virtually all of the bills discounted by commercial banks are commercial bills. Bills of exchange that arise out of commodity transactions are purchased by the bank at the face value less a deduction of interest for the period to maturity. Maturities of 90 days and 120 days are most common. Bills drawn by well-known corporations for the purchase of goods for resale are eligible for rediscounting at the Bank of Japan.

As noted earlier, the city banks lend relatively more of their funds to larger corporations. Some 64 percent of the city banks' loans and discounts, as compared to 39 percent of the regional banks', were to borrowers other than individuals and corporations with capitalization of less than

100 million yen ($333 thousand). Approximately one-fifth of the loans and discounts outstanding of all commercial banks (19 percent for city banks and 22 percent for regional banks) is for equipment purchases. The amount of equipment loans oustanding is about nine times as large as the value of corporate bonds held by all the commercial banks.

The Liabilities Side.   Corresponding to the fairly long-term nature of the commercial banks' asset structure is the equally long term of their deposits. Over one-half of the banks' deposits are time deposits, and of these, over three-quarters are for one year or longer. Of all the time deposits held at all types of banks (including trust banks and long-term credit banks), 46 percent was made by corporations, and the rest belonged to individuals. What emerges is a picture of commercial banks accepting largely medium-term savings deposits and making medium-term investment loans to business firms.

It is on the liabilities side that the difference between the city and regional banks is pronounced. While the regional banks raise most of their funds in the form of deposits (84 percent in 1974), the city banks rely significantly on the loans from the Bank of Japan and funds obtained in the money markets as the secondary sources of funds.[d] The city banks raise only about two-thirds (64 percent in 1974) of their funds in deposits. As noted earlier, the city banks' heavy use of these external sources of funds is a by-product of the rapid growth of the Japanese economy and the attendant massive demands for funds by large corporations. As of the end of 1974, over $29 billion of the city banks' resources had been raised through these external channels, while only about half a billion dollars of the regional banks' funds had been thus raised.

Deposits.   Banks are not classified in Japan according to the kinds of deposits they primarily accept. All types of "banks," including mutual loan and savings banks and credit associations, accept all types of deposits. The only noticeable difference is that the proportion of time deposits is appreciably lower in commercial banks than in other types of financial institutions. Individuals deposit money in a bank largely as savings; their choice of a particular bank is often made primarily on the basis of the location of the bank office.

The following four major types of deposits exist in Japan. Most private financial institutions that accept business and individual deposits offer, as a rule, all four facilities.

Current deposits (*toza yokin*) correspond to the checking account deposits in the West. Deposits are payable on demand, normally only by

---

[d]The city banks' raising of funds in the money markets will be discussed later.

check. The use of this facility is limited largely to business firms. There is no interest paid on current accounts.

Ordinary deposits (futsu yokin) are payable on demand, but upon presentation of a passbook. Interest of 3 percent per annum was paid on these deposits as of September 1974. This facility is popular with individuals seeking an outlet for idle funds.

Deposits at notice (tsuchi yokin) can be withdrawn on two days' notice. Interest of 3.25 percent per annum was paid on these deposits. This account is used primarily by business firms for placing their temporary surplus funds.

Time deposits (teiki yokin) have different levels of interest paid according to the length of deposits. Interest rates applicable to time deposits at all types of banks as of September 1974 were as follows: 5.50 percent for 3 months, 6.75 percent for 6 months, 7.75 percent for one year, and 8.00 percent per annum for two-year deposits. Business firms hold their semiliquid assets largely in this form because of the lack of availability of short-term instruments comparable to the U. S. Treasury bills or certificates of deposits.

The percentage distribution, by value, of these four types of deposits at all banks (including trust banks and long-term credit banks) at the end of 1974 was as follows:

Current deposits	9.9 percent
Ordinary deposits	17.8
Deposits at notice	12.6
Time deposits	53.0
Others	6.7

The Low Liquidity Ratio. Aggressive lending by the city banks has resulted in the very low liquidity ratio (the sum of currency, deposits with others, and call loans divided by total deposits) and the very high loan ratio (the sum of loans and discounts divided by deposits) of these banks. The average liquidity ratio of the city banks in 1974 was 4 percent, as contrasted to 8 percent for the regional banks. The average liquidity ratio was 93 percent for the city banks and 82 percent for the regional banks. This phenomenon of excessive lending and the slim liquidity base of the city banks is known in Japan as an "overloan" condition. Overloan is a "superficial" problem created by "the institutional peculiarities and rigidities" of the Japanese financial arrangements.[5]

The excessive corporate demand for bank loans could be easily reduced by facilitating corporations' raising of medium and long-term capital by alternative avenues (for example, by allowing them to pay higher interest rates on their bond issues). The narrow liquidity base of the city banks could be remedied by allowing them to tap the medium-term savings more aggressively (for example, by allowing them to issue certificates of deposits), and by making the Bank of Japan supply a larger monetary base to the banking system (for example, by making it redis-count bills more generously). In other words, overloan in itself is not a problem. It is merely a symptom of the more basic problem of institu-tional rigidity—of the failure of the Japanese government to develop alternative channels of investible funds that could supplement or replace the overused facilities of the city banks.[6]

Financial Institutions for Small Businesses and Cooperatives

The mutual loan and savings banks (*sogo ginko*) are essentially small business and consumer finance companies that are authorized to do regular banking business on a regional basis. They are not allowed to lend to a business firm with 300 or more employees. Credit associations (*shinyo kinko*) are nonprofit financial cooperatives whose business is restricted to a given locality. Only small businesses (fewer than 300 employees) and individuals can become members. Lending is limited to members, but deposits can be accepted from nonmembers. Credit associ-ations also provide regular banking business to its members and depos-itors. Credit cooperatives (*shinyo kumiai*) are similar to credit associations, except that they cannot accept deposits from, or make loans to, nonmem-bers. They are usually formed by a neighborhood group, a group of workers in the same company, and in association with a small business trade association.

Agricultural cooperatives (*nogyo kyodo kumiai*) are multipurpose cooperatives organized at the village level. They serve as "banks" for farmers by accepting their savings deposits and making livelihood, modernization, and housing loans to them. The financial aspects of the agricultural cooperatives are coordinated by credit federations of agricul-tural cooperatives at the prefectural level, and by the Norin Chukin Bank at the national level. On the average, about half of the agricultural cooperatives' funds is deposited with the credit federations, and in turn about half of the federations' funds is deposited in the Norin Chukin Bank.

The Norin Chukin Bank (*Norin Chuo Kinko,* or the Central Coopera-tive Bank of Agriculture and Forestry) is a cooperative bank for agricul-tural cooperatives. Its capital is subscribed entirely by its affiliated or-ganizations. It accepts deposits from its member organizations, public bodies, and nonprofit organizations. It can issue debentures up to twenty times its capital and reserves. It can make long-term loans (with maturity of up to fifty years) to its affiliated organizations.

The Shoko Chukin Bank (*Shoko Kumiai Chuo Kinko,* or the Central Bank for Commercial and Industrial Cooperatives) is similarly a bank for commercial and industrial cooperatives and associations. It was established for the primary purpose of providing funds to cooperatives of small businesses. Part of its capital (62 percent in 1975) is subscribed by the government. In return, the government appoints its officers and supervises its activities. Deposits can be accepted from its member organizations, public bodies, and other nonprofit organizations. It can also issue debentures up to twenty times the size of its capital and reserves. Loans of up to twenty years' maturity can be made to its member organizations and related enterprises.

Government Financial Institutions

In Chapter 5 we briefly noted the nature of the two special public banks—the Japan Development Bank and the Export–Import Bank of Japan—and the ten public corporations of loan and finance. As public corporations, their capital is subscribed entirely by the government, and their activities are highly regulated by the government.

The Japan Development Bank (JDB, *Nippon Kaihatsu Ginko*) was established in 1951 under the Japan Development Bank Law for the purpose of providing long-term loans for economic reconstruction and industrial development. The purpose of the bank is not to compete with private financial institutions, but is rather to supplement their resources by providing funds for investments in strategic industries for which private institutions' funds may be insufficient. The bank often makes loans jointly with private banks. The bank has made loans to marine transportation, electric power generation, railways, chemical, iron and steel, and machinery industries, as well as for urban and regional development, and for development of new technology. Its outstanding lending of about $9.5 billion at the end of 1974 was comparable to the amount of lending of a medium-sized city bank. The JDB has been the key nexus between the government fiscal funds and its industrial investments. At the end of 1974 the bank had, in addition to its government-subscribed capital of $780 million, borrowings from the government (predominantly from the Trust Fund) of $7.6 billion.

The Export–Import Bank of Japan (*Nippon Yushutsunyu Ginko*) was established in 1950. Its sources of funds, both capital and borrowing, are entirely public. It provides medium and long-term loans for the financing of exports of ships, rolling stock, plants and equipment. Over a half of its export financing has been made to the shipbuilding industry. The bank also makes loans for financing imports of key commodities, and financing overseas investments. Additionally, it makes direct loans to foreign governments for financing their imports of plants and equipment from Japan.

The common characteristics of the loan and finance corporations are that (1) they are established for the purpose of making specialized loans that private financial institutions find difficult to make, (2) their sources of funds are government-subscribed capital and borrowing from the government, and (3) they are authorized to issue debentures for the purpose of raising additional funds. Together with the two special public banks, the ten public corporations of loan and finance channel a significant part of investible funds from the public sector to the private sector (see Chapter 10).

The Money and Capital Markets

In this chapter we have thus far examined the basic flows of loanable funds in the economy, and the financial institutions that channel these flows. In this section, we focus our attention on the financial *markets,* where different financial institutions participate in dealing with different types of funds. Financial markets comprise the money market and the capital market. The former consists of the call-loan market and the bill-discount market, and the latter is divided into the bond market and the equities market.

The Call-Money Market

The call-loan market allows financial institutions to make adjustments in their liquidity positions. Those with temporary surplus funds can lend them to other institutions that are temporarily short of cash. This market thus closely resembles the federal funds market in the United States.

Loans are transacted largely through the call-loan dealers, of which there are six. Borrowers give promissory notes secured by a collateral. Virtually all of call loans are now of the "unconditional" type; after two days, the loan could be called or repaid on one day's notice. Over-the-month money that had been popular before June 1972 was abolished and replaced by the newly created bill-discount market (see next subsection).

The city banks are the principal borrowers in the call-money market. They absorb about 80 percent of the available funds. The net lenders are the regional banks, trust banks, mutual loan and savings banks, and other nonbank financial intermediaries, including credit associations and insurance companies. The city banks' voracious appetite for funds keeps the call-loan rates high. Between 1956 and 1974, the rate on the unconditionals ranged from 3.65 percent to 21.90 percent per annum. The rates are determined, on the whole, by the forces of supply and demand. They therefore serve as a good barometer of the general tightness or ease of credit. During periods of tight credit, the rates are typically above 12 percent; periods of excess liquidity may cause the rate to fall below the 5 percent mark. When the rates are high, the lending institutions tend to regard the call-money market as a place to make profitable and safe loans rather than a temporary outlet for their idle funds.

The Bill-Discount Market

The bill-discount market was established by the Bank of Japan in May 1971. This market provides a channel for short-term funds that have somewhat longer maturity (up to three months) than call money.

In Japan, the market for third-party discounting of ordinary commercial bills is virtually nonexistent because of the traditional reluctance of the banks to part with their customers' bills. In the context of the insider–outsider psychology of Japanese society, transferring the customers' liabilities to other parties would somehow smack of betraying the trust and confidence the customers have in the bank. Besides, that would reveal to other banks the nature of transactions between the bank and its customers. Consequently, the overwhelming majority of the bills that are discounted in the new bill-discount market is either bills drawn by corporations on banks and accepted by them or bills drawn by banks on themselves on the security of commercial bills they have previously discounted. In either case, the bills become the banks' liabilities when "sold" to the third party (see Table 9–4). The bill-discount market in Japan is therefore not exactly the same as the commercial bill-discount markets in the West; rather, it resembles more closely the American bankers' acceptances market.

The bill-discount market is similar to the call-money market in many respects. Transactions are conducted through the same six call-loan dealers. The city banks are principal issuers (sellers) of bills, and the same institutions that lend in the call-loan market are the net buyers of bills. As of the end of 1974, the city banks had an outstanding bill balance of $16.76 billion (see Table 9–4), which was 98 percent of the total bills outstanding. The regional banks, trust banks, and credit associations were the most active buyers (lenders) in 1974.

The Bank of Japan's "open" market operation to regulate the money supply now works through this market. In June 1972, the BOJ began purchases of bills from the call-loan dealers. Between December 1972 and December 1973, the Bank's holding of "bills bought" increased by $11 billion, while during the same period the city banks' "bills sold" outstanding increased by $8.3 billion. As of the end of 1974, the Bank's holding of bills constituted 82 percent of the total bills outstanding.[7]

The Bond Market

Table 9–5 shows the relative importance of the different types of financing in supplying industrial funds. Whereas internal financing provides 44 percent and borrowings from private banks supply 28 percent of the funds, the bond market contributes less than 2 percent. Table 9–6 indicates who held how much of different types of bonds and debentures as of March 31, 1970. The financial institutions, including the Bank of Japan, were the most important holders of bonds, accounting for 59 percent of total bonds outstanding, of which the banks' share was 30 percent. Of the public sector's holding of $12.1 billion (18 percent of total), $11.9 billion were held by the national government, practically all of which were in the Trust Fund Special Account.

In the postwar period until 1966, the government had strictly adhered to the balanced-budget principle. This principle was revoked in 1966 to

Table 9–5
Average Annual Net Supply of Industrial Funds, by Source, 1965–1974

Types of Financing	Amount (billions of dollars)[a]	Percentage Distribution
Shares	$2.4	3.3%
Corporate debentures	1.3	1.8
Loans from private financial institutions[b]	34.0	46.7
(of which banks)[c]	(20.6)	(28.3)
Loans from government financial institutions[b]	3.0	4.2
Depreciation[d]	21.7	29.8
Retained earnings[d]	10.3	14.2
Total	72.7	100.0

Source: Bank of Japan, Statistics Department, *Economic Statistics Annual, 1974,* pp. 43–44 and 74.
[a]The yen figures for all years are converted at the rate of $1 = ¥300.
[b]Include discounts.
[c]Both banking and trust accounts of all banks.
[d]Averages of 1965–73.

Table 9–6

Holdings of Bonds and Debentures, End of March 1970

(Billions of Dollars)

			Holders		
Types of Bonds	Financial Institutions	Public Sector[a]	Corporate Business	Persons[b]	Total
Short-term government bills	$2.7	$3.2	$0.1	$0.0[c]	$6.0
Government bonds	6.6	1.9	0.1	1.2	9.8
Local government bonds	4.3	0.0[c]	0.1	0.1	4.5
Public corporation bonds	7.7	5.4	2.1	3.1	18.3
Bank debentures	9.0	1.4	1.2	6.7	18.3
Corporate debentures	8.3	0.2	0.1	0.5	9.1
Total	38.6	12.1	3.7	11.6	66.0

Source: L. S. Pressnell, ed., *Money and Banking in Japan*, Bank of Japan, Economic Research Department, trans. S. Nishimura (New York: St. Martin's Press, 1973), p. 433.

[a]Includes the national and local governments, and public corporations.

[b]Include noncorporate business.

[c]Less than $50 million.

counter that year's recession, and long-term government bonds were issued for the first time since the end of the war. The general-account deficit bonds have been issued every year since then. Private financial institutions absorb the bulk of these bonds; their placement with the Bank of Japan is prohibited by law. Short-term government bills include the Treasury bills and other bills issued to cover deficits in several special accounts (e.g., foodstuffs control bills to cover subsidies on rice). These bills are sold principally to the Bank of Japan.

Local government bonds are issued with approvals of the central government, which each year formulates the local bond floatation plan as part of its fiscal investment and loan program (see Chapter 10). Most of the public corporation bonds are guaranteed by the government as to the principal and the payment of interests. Bank debentures, as noted earlier, are issued by the long-term credit banks and the few other special banks. Small denomination discount debentures of one-year maturity are bought almost exclusively by individuals. These debentures provide individual savers with opportunities to earn interests higher than those paid on time deposits. Interest-bearing bank debentures of five-year maturity are purchased primarily by financial institutions.

Corporate debentures are held mainly by financial institutions, largely banks. Individual ownership of corporate debentures is increasing lately. The proportion of new debenture issues bought by individuals increased from about one-fifth in 1968 to over one-half in 1974.

By government policy, the rates on new issues of all types of bonds are kept rigidly low. During the last twenty years, the yields on newly issued corporate debentures have ranged between 7 and 8 percent, and the yield on government bonds, first issued in 1966, has been about 0.75 percent lower. The purpose of this policy is to keep the cost of borrowing low for both government and private borrowers. The low-interest policy, however, has a serious distorting effect on the financial market. Except for periods of excessive liquidity, new bond rates tend to be below the market-clearing levels. It is a matter of basic economics that, whenever a disequilibrium of this sort exists, some form of rationing must be used. Otherwise, the demand for funds (the supply of bonds) would exceed the supply of funds (the demand for bonds). This rationing is provided by the government regulating the timing and the volume of new bond issues. The Ministry of Finance and the Bank of Japan jointly determine ceilings on corporate debenture issues on a quarterly basis. Floatation of corporate debentures must be approved by these agencies on a case-by-case basis within the quarterly ceilings.

When the yields on new bond issues are lower than the yields prevailing in the secondary markets, not only must the demand for funds be curtailed, but also the supply of funds (the demand for bonds) must be artificially generated. The problem is especially acute in the case of government bonds whose new-issue yields are lower than the yields on other types of bonds. The price of the bond is therefore likely to fall after it is issued, reflecting the yields prevailing in the secondary market. The holders of the bond will consequently be forced to keep the bond until maturity in order to avoid incurring a capital loss. Understandably, the public is reluctant to purchase new issues of government bonds. The government is thus compelled to administratively allocate underwriting of government bonds among financial institutions. More than 90 percent of government bonds are bought under duress by financial institutions. The 1974 share in the compulsory subscription of government bonds by the city, trust, and long-term credit banks was 49 percent.[8]

The Equities Market

As noted earlier (Table 9–5), new stock issues raised only 3.3 percent of Japan's business funds between 1965 and 1974. This amounted to about 5.9 percent of total external financing, as contrasted to 50.5 percent raised through bank loans.

In Japan, the securities business is strictly separated from commercial banking. Licensed securities companies engage in the following four categories of business: selling and buying of securities for their own accounts as dealers, selling and buying of securities for their customers as brokers, underwriting new issues of securities, and handling public offerings of securities. Trading in existing stocks constitutes the bulk of the securities companies' business.

The secondary stock trading markets are the only "open" markets in the Japanese financial system in the sense that a large and indefinite number of parties participate in them, and prices are determined by the forces of supply and demand. There are eight stock exchanges in Japan, the largest being the Tokyo Stock Exchange (TSE). Having been established in 1878, the TSE is now the second largest stock exchange in the world. In 1974, 1,390 companies were listed on the two sections of the TSE. Stocks are traded by the 260 securities companies, of which the largest four are Nomura Securities, Nikko Securities, Daiwa Securities, and Yamaichi Securities.

Stock ownership is widely diffused. At the end of 1973, 13 percent of the Japanese personal financial assets, as compared to 32 percent in the United States, were in stocks.[9] About 6 percent of the Japanese own stocks, as compared to about 15 percent of the U.S. population.[10]

Table 9–7 shows the changing composition of stock ownership from 1960 to 1972. The relative importance of individuals diminished, and that

Table 9–7
Percentage Distribution of the Ownership of Listed Stocks, Selected Years

Stockholders	1960	1968	1972
Financial institutions	23.1%	30.3%	33.8%
Investment trusts	7.5	1.7	1.3
Securities companies	3.7	2.1	1.8
Business corporations	17.8	21.4	26.6
Foreign corporations	1.1	2.1	3.4
Individuals	46.6	42.1	32.9
Others	0.2	0.3	0.2
Total	100.0	100.0	100.0

Source: Nikkei Business Henshu-bu, *Nihon no Kigyo Kankyo* [The environment of Japanese business] (Tokyo: Nihon Keizai Shinbun-sha, 1974), p. 35.

of financial and business corporations increased. The rising corporate ownership of stocks is not unrelated to the recently intensifying tendency of grouping in Japan's industrial structure.

Monetary Policy

Monetary policy, the regulation of business activities through alteration in the availability and cost of credit, is within the competence of the Ministry of Finance and its operational agency, the Bank of Japan. The latter is independent from the MOF in name only. Basically, in all matters related to money and credit, the ministry calls the tune. The Bank of Japan fulfills operational responsibilities in monetary matters within the broader framework of fundamental policy established by the ministry.

The Bank of Japan

The Bank of Japan (BOJ) was established in 1882 under the old Bank of Japan Law as the central bank of the nation, with an exclusive authority to issue bank notes. It was reorganized in 1942 under the current Bank of Japan Law. Technically, it is a private corporation in which the government holds 55 percent of the shares and the private subscribers hold the rest. There is no general meeting of shareholders, and they in no way participate in the management of the bank.

The BOJ is administered by an executive board consisting of the governor, vice-governor, and three or more executive directors. The governor and the vice-governor are appointed by the cabinet, and the executive directors are appointed by the Minister of Finance from among the list of persons recommended by the governor.

The highest organ of the Bank is the Policy Board, consisting of seven members: the governor, two government representatives (one each from the Finance Ministry and the Economic Planning Agency), and four members (each representing the city banks, regional banks, commerce and industry, and agriculture) appointed by the cabinet and confirmed by both houses of the Diet. The two government representatives have no voting rights. The chairman of the board is elected from among the voting members. Within the competence of the Policy Board are the following matters: the lending policy, "open" market operations, determining the reserve requirements, determining the Bank Rate, and establishing the Bank of Japan guidelines (within the statutory maxima) on the loan and deposit rates of private financial institutions. In changing the reserve requirements, however, the Policy Board must obtain an approval of the Finance Minister. Furthermore, although changing the Bank Rate is an authority vested with the Policy Board under the Bank of Japan Law, it is never done without close coordination and consultation with the MOF's Banking Bureau.

The law establishing the Ministry of Finance states that the ministry "supervises the Bank of Japan." The Bank of Japan Law itself vests the ministry with extensive supervisory authority over the Bank. In the late 1950s, a battle was waged between the Bank of Japan and the Ministry of Finance over a reform of the Bank of Japan Law. The Bank wanted greater independence from the ministry. It wanted to have total control over monetary policy matters, and to have the ministry's authority limited to that of requesting a delay or reconsideration of a Bank's decision. Although the zaikai strongly supported the Bank's position, the reform attempt was unsuccessful in the face of the strong opposition from the MOF officials.[11]

Instruments of Monetary Policy

The central bank loan and discount policy, the reserve requirement policy, and the open market operations are the three standard instruments of monetary policy listed in every economics textbook. In practice, the relative importance and effectiveness of these measures vary from country to country, depending on the country's historical and institutional circumstances. In Japan, the primary instrument is the loan and discount policy; the other two play supplementary roles at best. Changes in the availability and cost of credit are effected principally by the BOJ's alterations in its lending policy, supplemented by the uniquely Japanese practice of the Bank's restrictive guidance on commercial banks' lending to their customers.

The Reserve Requirement Policy. The Bank of Japan determines the required ratios of reserves[e] against different types of deposits, subject to approval by the Finance Minister. Although the statutory maximum of the reserve ratio is 20 percent, actual ratios are set much lower. The reserve ratios must be kept low because of the perpetual shortages of funds of the city banks. Compulsory deposits with the BOJ at no interest is naturally very unpopular among the bankers. When the actual reserve deposits fall short of the legal requirement, the financial institution must pay to the Bank, as a penalty, a sum equal to the shortage multiplied by a rate which is 3.75 percent per annum higher than the basic Bank Rate.

The legal reserve ratios in force for banks as of February 1, 1976, were as follows: For time deposits in excess of $5 billion, 1.75 percent; between $1 billion and $5 billion, 0.75 percent; below $1 billion, 0.25 percent. On deposits other than time deposits, the required reserve ratios for the three deposit categories were: 3.00 percent, 1.75 percent, and 0.75 percent, respectively. By way of comparison, the highest reserve requirements for large U. S. banks in effect as of February 29, 1976, were 6 percent against time deposits and 16.5 percent on demand deposits.

The changes in the reserve ratios required against the city banks' time deposits between January 1973 and February 1976 were as follows:

January 1973	1.00 percent
March 1973	1.50
June 1973	1.75
September 1973	2.00
January 1974	2.25
November 1975	2.00
February 1976	1.75

The February 1976 reduction of the reserve ratios against all types of deposits was estimated to free about $1.3 billion of the compulsory reserve deposits of $6.6 billion.[12] The released reserve could eventually result in a much larger increase in the nation's money supply, as explained in every economics textbook. The control of reserve ratios could thus be a very potent weapon of monetary control, particularly if larger changes were allowed. As noted earlier, reserve ratios have been kept at very low levels, and their changes have been moderate. It appears that the Bank of Japan is content with using this potentially powerful weapon as a supplementary tool, at least for the time being.

Market Operations. Open market operations as practiced in the United

---

[e]Only the deposits with the Bank of Japan are counted as reserves; cash on hand is not.

States and Great Britain are not feasible in Japan, since there are effectively no *open* markets for bonds and bills. In the 1960s, the Bank of Japan began supplying reserves to the banking system by direct purchases of government and public corporation bonds from financial institutions on a compulsory assignment basis. These operations have come to be known as the "market operations" of the BOJ. Since the market for bonds was thin, free bidding could not be used to determine the purchase price. The BOJ therefore used the price prevailing in the (thin) market, thereby preventing the purchase operations from causing sharp rises in bond prices. The inception of the bill-discount market in 1971 provided the BOJ with another avenue of channeling reserves into the system. In June 1972, it began purchasing commercial bills from the call-loan dealers. Market operations in bonds were discontinued at that time. By the end of 1974, the Bank's holding of purchased bills had approached $14 billion (see Table 9–8).

The Lending Policy.   The lending policy of the Bank of Japan is the monetary policy par excellence. Because of the extremely strong demand of the banks for loans and discounts from the BOJ, and the very heavy reliance of business firms on bank loans, changes in the cost and availability of BOJ credit have pronounced effects on the total volume of credit, and through it, on business activities.

The Bank of Japan periodically announces changes in the rates of discount and loans known as the Bank Rates (*kotei buai*). Since October 1972, there have been two such rates. One is the rate of discount of commercial bills and rate of interest on loans secured by government bonds. This rate is commonly referred to as *the* Bank Rate, and is

Table 9–8
The Balance Sheet of the Bank of Japan, End of 1974
(Billions of Dollars)

Assets		Liabilities and Net Worth	
Gold bullion	$0.1	Bank notes issued	$38.9
Cash	0.2	Financial institutions' deposits	6.6
Bills discounted	0.4	Government deposits	0.4
Loans	5.2	Other liabilities	1.3
Bills bought	13.9	Capital, reserves, and surpluses	2.8
Government securities	17.5		
Other securities	0.6		
Foreign accounts	11.6		
Other assets	0.5		
Total	50.1	Total	50.1

Source: Bank of Japan, Statistics Department, *Economic Statistics Annual, 1974*, pp. 27–28.

considered as the benchmark of the cost of credit. The other is the rate of interest on loans secured by other types of collateral; this rate is kept 0.25 percent higher than the basic Bank Rate.

During the inflation/recession period of 1972–75, the Bank Rate was first raised and then lowered in several steps, as indicated below:

April 1972	4.25 percent
April 1973	5.00
May 1973	5.50
July 1973	6.00
August 1973	7.00
December 1973	9.00
April 1975	8.50
June 1975	8.00
August 1975	7.50
October 1975	6.50

As the Bank Rate was lowered from its peak of 9.00 percent in December 1973 to 7.50 percent in August 1975 in three steps, somewhere between 60 and 70 percent of the reduction was passed onto business borrowers, and the remaining portion was absorbed by the banks.[13] This indicates that changes in the Bank Rate fall largely on business firms as changes in their cost of credit. Because of the heavy reliance of Japanese business firms on bank loans, small changes in their cost of credit have magnified effects on the level of business activities.

Window Guidance. Window guidance (*madoguchi kisei*) is a form of administrative guidance employed by the Bank of Japan to restrict the volume of financial institutions' lending during periods of monetary tightness. Although ostensibly billed as an informal guidance, in fact it is an extremely effective instrument of monetary control. Every three months the Bank establishes the maximum amount of loans and discounts each bank can grant during the next three months. The quotas are based on the actual lending record of each bank in the same quarter of the preceding year. Originally applied only to the city banks, it is now extended to the trust banks and the long-term credit banks. During the past periods of extreme monetary restriction, the guidance was also extended to other types of financial institutions.

Window guidance is a form of credit rationing, and as do many other methods of rationing, it obviates or reduces the need to rely on the price (interest rate) to do the rationing. Under this system, larger corporate borrowers generally can expect a steady supply of low-cost funds from their city banks. The banks must reduce, however, the volume of their total lending. They naturally decrease or eliminate their loans to smaller, nonkeiretsu borrowers. Group affiliations and personal ties become important factors in deciding who get the money.

Just as banks wield power over business because of the latter's reliance on bank loans, the Bank of Japan wields power over the banks, particularly the city banks, because of the latter's heavy reliance on the financial resources of the Bank. A comparison of Tables 9–4 and 9–8 reveals that, as of the end of 1974, the city banks owed the Bank nearly $19 billion in the forms of loans and sold bills. Thus, while the city bank managers consider the BOJ's window guidance as a cumbersome encroachment upon their managerial prerogatives, they have few alternatives but to abide by it.

Notes

1. For further information on money and banking in Japan, see Ryoichi Mikitani, "Monetary Policy in Japan," in Karl Holbik, ed., *Monetary Policy in Twelve Industrial Countries* (Boston: Federal Reserve Bank of Boston, 1973); L. S. Pressnell, ed., *Money and Banking in Japan,* Bank of Japan, Economic Research Department, trans. S. Nishimura (New York: St. Martin's Press, 1973); Hugh Patrick and Henry Rosovsky, eds., *Asia's New Giant* (Washington, D.C.: The Brookings Institution, 1976), chaps. 3–4; Wilbur F. Monroe, *Japan: Financial Markets and the World Economy* (New York: Praeger Publishers, 1973), chap. 8; and Bank of Japan, Economic Research Department, *The Bank of Japan: Its Organization and Monetary Policies* (Tokyo: The Bank of Japan, 1973). The most useful statistical information on the Japanese financial system is found in Bank of Japan, Statistics Department, *Economics Statistics Annual.*

2. Nikkei Business Henshu-bu, *Nihon no Kigyo Kankyo* [The environment of Japanese business] (Tokyo: Nihon Keizai Shinbun-sha, 1974), p. 29 and Economic Planning Agency, *Keizai Hakusho, showa 50-nen ban* [Economic white paper, 1975] (Tokyo: Ministry of Finance, Printing Bureau, 1975), app. p. 43.

3. Henry C. Wallich and Mable I. Wallich, "Banking and Finance," in Patrick and Rosovsky, *Asia's New Giant,* chap. 4, p. 269.

4. Bank of Japan, *Economic Statistics Annual, 1974.*

5. Wallich and Wallich in *Asia's New Giant,* pp. 289–290.

6. For an incisive analysis of the "overloan problem," see ibid., pp. 284–290.

7. Bank of Japan, *Economic Statistics Annual, 1974,* pp. 27–28 and 75–76.

8. *Mainichi Shinbun,* 24 August 1975.

9. The relative importance of savings deposits is reversed between the two countries: 65 percent in Japan and 28 percent in the United States. Wallich and Wallich in *Asia's New Giant*, p. 277, table 4–7.

10. Monroe, *Japan,* p. 121.

11. For details of the battle between the BOJ and the MOF over the reform of the Bank of Japan Law, see Frank C. Langdon, "Big Business Lobbying in Japan: The Case of Central Bank Reform," *American Political Science Review* 55 (September 1961): 527–538.

12. *Asahi Shinbun,* 20 January 1976.

13. *Nihon Keizai Shinbun,* 24 October 1975.

10 The Fiscal System and Fiscal Policy

Fiscal Policy

In many of the market-oriented, industrially developed economies of the world, monetary policy and fiscal policy are regarded as twin instruments of managing aggregate demand. Working in tandem, they presumably help stabilize output, employment, and prices. In Japan, for historical and institutional reasons, the task of short-run economic stabilization is assumed almost exclusively by monetary policy. By *zaisei seisaku* ("fiscal policy") is meant the management of taxation and public expenditures with a view toward achieving broader socioeconomic goals—balanced growth and development of the national economy for a better quality of national life.

That the government's fiscal activities affect economic conditions of the nation is of course fully realized. From time to time a large and stimulative budget is prepared to supplement the recession-fighting effect of monetary policy. Government spending, particularly public work expenditures, are often stepped up or postponed to smooth out business cycles. On the whole, however, the Japanese government has so far made limited use of the budget as a tool of short-run demand management. A sound fiscal policy, as perceived in Japan, calls for keeping tax revenues and government expenditures balanced under all but extremely serious circumstances. Variations in taxes and expenditures are to be made to conform to the availability and cost of credit so that fiscal and monetary policies do not work at cross-purposes. The relatively unaggressive use of fiscal policy as a countercyclical tool has not been regarded as a deficiency in Japan partly because monetary policy is extremely effective in regulating aggregate demand, and partly because the government's investment and lending activities (FILP) outside the regular budget channels can be managed flexibly as a tool of stabilization, as we shall see later in the chapter.

Taxation[1]

Throughout the postwar period, the combined tax revenue of both the national and local governments has been slightly less than 20 percent of national income. In 1973, the ratio rose to 22 percent. These figures are

171

172

considerably lower than the comparable ratios for the United States and the Western European countries, except Italy, as seen in Table 10–1.

As for sources of tax revenue, we can see from Table 10–2 that Japan raises a substantial portion (65 percent) of its total tax revenue from income taxes. The second largest source of revenue is the host of taxes on the consumption of goods and services. These taxes are levied on liquor, gasoline, and selected consumer durables. There is no general sales tax in Japan.

The Budget

An International Comparison

A comparison of the size and composition of government expenditures of the United States, the United Kingdom, and Japan for 1972 is shown in Table 10–3. The total government expenditure in Japan is about one-fifth of its gross domestic product (GDP), as compared to about one-third in both the United States and the United Kingdom. From this we may conclude that, at least quantitatively, the role which the government plays in the nation's economic life is relatively smaller in Japan than in either the United States or the United Kingdom. This conclusion may not be totally warranted since the Japanese government's "deficiency" lies almost exclusively in defense and welfare expenditures. On government investment, it spends relatively more than the American or British government. Japan's percentage expenditure on defense (0.9 percent of GDP) is materially lower than the international average. Another important factor is the relatively small welfare-related expenditures. If we combine

Table 10–1
Tax Burden as Percentage of National Income, Selected Countries, 1973

Country	National Taxes	Local Taxes	Total
United Kingdom	30.7%	4.7%	35.3%
West Germany	27.3	4.2	31.5
United States	16.7	11.9	28.6
France	25.0	3.0	28.0
Japan	15.3	7.1	22.4
Italy	19.8	1.5	21.4

Source: Ministry of Local Autonomy, *Chiho Zaisei Hakusho, showa 50-nen ban* [Local finance white paper, 1975] (Tokyo: Ministry of Finance, Printing Bureau, 1975), pp. 208–209.

Table 10–2
Percentage Distribution of Tax Revenues, Fiscal 1973

Tax Source	National Taxes	Local Taxes	Total
Individual income tax	24.3%	10.8%[a]	35.1%
Corporate income tax	21.5	8.1[b]	29.6
Inheritance tax	2.0		2.0
Property taxes		5.4	5.4
Taxes on goods and services	19.4	8.5	27.9
Total	67.1	32.9	100.0

Source: Bank of Japan, Statistics Department, *Economic Statistics Annual, 1974,* pp. 185 and 191.
[a]Prefectural and municipal inhabitants' taxes.
[b]Prefectural business tax.

the three "welfare" expenditures (health and medicine, social security and welfare, and government transfer payments to persons), we obtain the following results:

United States	9.7 percent of GDP
United Kingdom	15.2
Japan	6.0

The difference between the U.S.–U.K. average (12.5 percent) and the Japanese figure (6.0 percent) is 6.5 percent, which is larger than the comparable difference in defense expenditures.

Table 10–3
International Comparison of Government Expenditures as Percentages of Gross Domestic Product, 1972

	United States	United Kingdom	Japan
Government consumption			
General public services	3.1%	2.7%	2.5%
Defense	6.4	4.9	0.9
Education	5.1	3.9	3.3
Health and medicine	0.3	3.9	0.6
Social security and welfare	1.2	0.9	0.6
Other services	2.8	2.5	1.5
Subtotal	19.0	18.7	9.4
Government investment	3.3	4.7	6.4
Subsidies to businesses	0.5	1.9	1.0
Transfer payments to persons	8.2	10.4	4.8
Total	31.0	35.7	21.6

Source: *Nihon Keizai Shinbun,* 1 September 1975.

In contrast to the relative paucity of spending on defense and welfare, the Japanese government plays a relatively larger role than its American or British counterpart in the nation's capital formation, as the following figures for government investment as percentages of total government expenditures show:

United States	10.6 percent
United Kingdom	13.2
Japan	30.0

The Types of Budget

The Japanese government must prepare the following three budgets and submit them to the Diet for approval: the general account budget, the special accounts budget, and the public corporations accounts budget. The broad policy objectives and priorities in the budgets are determined by the Ministry of Finance officials. The ministry's Budget Bureau is principally responsible for the allocation of funds. At the final stage of budget formulation, the ministers and the majority party leaders engage in tough negotiations with the key Budget Bureau officials over allocations of special concern to their constituencies.[2] Local government budgets are consolidated at the national level and submitted to the Diet for reference.

The general account expenditures include most basic current expenditures of the government. The bulk of the national tax revenue goes into this account. In addition to taxes, the profits of the government monopoly and government enterprises are included in the general account revenues. The proceeds from the sales of long-term government bonds also go into the general account.

Special accounts are designed for programs that are not convenient or appropriate to be included in the general account. The common characteristic of the forty-one special accounts is the need to match revenues with expenditures. This need arises when the government operates an enterprise (e.g., postal service), manages a fund (e.g., national pensions, foreign exchanges, etc.), or earmarks tax revenues for a special project or program (e.g., earmarking gasoline tax for road improvements). The government is also required to submit to the Diet the budgets of the fifteen public corporations because of their importance in the national economy and their heavy reliance on public funds. These public corporations include the three *kosha* ("public service" corporations), the ten *koko* (loan and finance corporations), and the two special public banks.

The scale of Japan's public finance proper can be best measured by combining the general account budget and the local government budgets. The following figures represent the 1974 budgeted expenditures:[3]

Central government general account expenditures	$57.0 billion
+ Local governments' expenditures	57.9
− Central government's grants-in-aid to local governments	(27.2)
= Net governmental expenditures	87.7

It may be noted that there is a considerable amount of overlapping between the central and local government expenditures. Of the general account expenditures totaling $57 billion, $27.2 billion (48 percent) were payments made to local governments. Of this amount, $12.1 billion were designated as "local allocations." These represent part of the national tax revenue which the central government shares with local governments on the basis of the financial needs of each locality. Allocations are made to equalize the quality of public services throughout the country. Local governments are allowed to spend these moneys with no strings attached. The remaining $15.1 billion were "categorical grants" (subsidies, etc.), the uses for which are specified in detail by the central government. Payments for local construction projects and subsidies for education are the two largest items of categorical grants.

The intergovernmental grants-in-aid of $27.2 billion in the 1974 budget amounted to 47 percent of the local governments' budget revenues for that year. The percentage distribution of the local government revenues was as follows:[4]

Taxes	41.4 percent
Local allocations	20.9
Categorical grants	26.1
Bond proceeds	5.9
Others	5.7

Table 10–4 gives a breakdown of the fiscal 1975 general account budget by principal items. Note that the local allocations are shown as a separate item, but the categorical grants are not. The latter are contained in the other expense items, notably public works, and education and science.

The Fiscal Investment and Loan Program

In addition to the three budgets, the government must submit to the Diet each year its Fiscal Investment and Loan Program (FILP, *zaisei toyushi keikaku*). The FILP is basically an annual governmental plan for allocat-

176

Table 10–4
The General Account Budget, Fiscal 1975

Principal Items	Value ($ billions)	Percentage Distribution
Revenues		
Taxes and stamps	$57.8	81.5%
Others	4.2	5.9
Bond proceeds	6.7	9.4
Carried-over surplus	2.3	3.3
Total revenues	71.0	100.0
Expenditures		
Social security expenses	13.1	18.5
Education and science	8.8	12.4
National debt expenses	3.5	4.9
Pensions	2.5	3.6
Local tax allocations	14.8	20.8
Defense expenses	4.4	6.2
Public works	9.7	13.7
Foodstuffs control expenses	3.0	4.3
Others	11.2	15.7
Total expenditures	71.0	100.0

Source: *Nihon Keizai Shinbun,* 1 January 1976.

ing its Trust Fund's surpluses as long-term, low-interest loans to government-affiliated organizations and local governments. Each year the government receives large amounts of funds in its pension, annuity, insurance, and savings programs. These funds are entrusted to the government, and as such should not be spent by it as current expenditures. Instead, the funds are placed in the special accounts (the Trust Fund Special Account and the Postal Life Insurance and Annuity Special Account), and made available to public corporations and local governments as loans and investments.[a] Table 10–5 shows the sources of funds and their uses in the fiscal 1975 Fiscal Investment and Loan Program.

We see from the table that in the FILP, funds are transferred primarily from the Trust Fund to public corporations and local governments. Within the Trust Fund, the largest sources of funds are the deposits of postal savings and the contributions to the national welfare insurance. Among the public corporations, the eight largest borrowers were:

Japan National Railways	$3.1 billion
Housing Loan Corporation	3.1
Japan Housing Corporation	2.2
People's Finance Corporation	2.1
Export–Import Bank of Japan	2.1

[a]The term "investment" is used here in the sense of acquiring financial assets, not *real* investment in buildings, equipment, and inventories of goods.

Table 10–5
Fiscal Investment and Loan Program, Fiscal 1975
(Billions of Dollars)

	Sources of Funds		
Uses of Funds	Trust Fund Special Account	PLIA[a] Special Account	Total
Special accounts	$0.5	$0.1	$0.6
Public corporations	20.9[b]	2.2	23.1
Local governments	4.5	1.2	5.7
Special private banks and corporations	0.2	0.1	0.3
Total	26.2[b]	3.5	29.7

Source: *Nihon Keizai Shinbun,* 1 January 1976.
[a] Postal Life Insurance and Annuity.
[b] Includes $0.2 billion from the Industrial Investment Special Account.

Japan Highway Corporation	2.0
Small Business Finance Corporation	1.9
Japan Development Bank	1.5

The total loans and investments to these eight public corporations ($18 billion) amounted to 61 percent of all the FILP lending in fiscal 1975. These corporations in turn lent the funds to their clients, including home buyers, small businessmen, and farmers. Here we observe that the Japanese government is playing the role of a very important financial intermediary. It absorbs people's savings through postal savings, insurance and pension programs, etc., and channels these funds back to the private sector, via public loan and finance corporations, as various forms of low-cost loans.

Although the FILP is basically a financial process, its size and composition cannot leave the real economy unaffected. For example, the money lent to the Japan Housing Corporation and the Housing Loan Corporation is bound to result in more homes being built and purchased. The fiscal 1975 allocations of the FILP funds by their end use were as follows:[5]

Housing	$6.6 billion
Small businesses	4.8
Improvement of living environment	4.8
Transportation and communication	3.7
Economic aid and promotion of international trade	2.4
Highways	2.2

| Education and welfare | 2.0 |
| Agriculture, forestry, and fisheries | 1.3 |

In the early postwar years, the FILP funds were allocated preferentially to the four key strategic industries (electric power generation, coal mining, steel, and shipping) by way of the Japan Development Bank. The emphasis has been shifting toward social overhead capital and social welfare, as the foregoing figures indicate.

Although the Finance Ministry formulates the FILP and oversees its management, and the public corporations carry out the actual allocations of loans and investments, the other ministries and agencies are not without influence over who get the funds. The FILP funds which are made available to public corporations are *assigned* to ministries and agencies according to their jurisdictions. The ministries are authorized to determine the maximum amounts of loans to be made for each category, and the interest rate to be charged in each category. The recommendations of the ministries as to who should actually receive loans in each category are highly respected by the public corporations. This power of mediating loans enables the ministries and agencies to wield considerable influence over the industries and firms under their wings.

The FILP has grown rapidly in recent years so that it is now over 40 percent as large as the general account budget. Fiscal investments and loans are important supplements to the general account expenditures for allocating resources to projects that have special social importance. For this reason, the FILP is often called the "second budget." One important advantage of the FILP over the ordinary government budget is the former's flexibility. The FILP is not a budget; it is merely a *plan* for leanding Trust Fund surpluses. In actually carrying out the lending program, the government is required to implement it flexibly, giving due consideration to the changing conditions of the economy and private finance. This flexibility of the FILP makes it an ideal instrument of aggregate demand management. When the monetary brake is applied on the economy, for example, the Trust Fund lending can be reduced to reinforce the effect of the tight money policy. Contrarily, the FILP lending to the more vulnerable sectors of the economy can be stepped up in order to soften the adverse impact of tight money on them.

The FILP constitutes a nexus between the fiscal and the financial; it is fiscal in form but financial in nature. In the Japanese economy we can identify three main flows of funds in addition to the basic income-consumption flow and the flow of business savings (retained earnings and depreciation). The first is the fiscal flow—that of taxes and bond proceeds spent as general account expenditures. The second is the financial flow of deposits in, and lending by, private financial institutions. The third is the fiscal/financial flow of the FILP. It channels private surpluses in the forms of postal savings deposits and social security contributions through the government's special accounts to public corporations and local authorities. A large portion of the funds is returned to the private sector in the form of loans made by public corporations. The Ministry of Finance oversees and regulates all three flows. The fiscal flow is the responsibility of the Budget Bureau; it draws up the budgets and controls their implementation. The Banking Bureau is in charge of the financial flow; it formulates monetary policy and supervises the Bank of Japan and other financial institutions. The ministry's Financial Bureau formulates the FILP and manages the Trust Fund.

Notes

1. For a fairly detailed account of the Japanese tax system, see Joseph A. Pechman and Keimei Kaizuka, "Taxation," in Hugh Patrick and Henry Rosovsky, eds., *Asia's New Giant* (Washington, D.C.: The Brookings Institution, 1976), chap. 5.

2. For details of budget preparation, see John C. Campbell, "Japanese Budget *Baransu*," in Ezra Vogel, ed., *Modern Japanese Organization and Decision-Making* (Berkeley and Los Angeles: University of California Press, 1975), pp. 71–100.

3. Economic Planning Agency, *Keizai Yoran, 1975* [Summary economic statistics, 1975] (Tokyo: Ministry of Finance, Printing Bureau, 1975), pp. 86–87.

4. Ibid.

5. *Nihon Keizai Shinbun,* 1 January 1976.

11 Concluding Remarks

In the preceding chapters we have examined the main features and general characteristics of the heartland of the Japanese economic scene. What emerges from this brief survey is a picture of a system of national economic and administrative management whose subsystems are organically connected to each other on a hierarchical principle without forming a sole center of power. The entire politicoeconomic complex is a "spiderless cobweb." The MITI regulates the industries, and the Finance Ministry controls the financial institutions. The business community's influence over politicians is derived from the power of the former's money. The higher bureaucrats are sensitive to the wishes of the politicians and the business leaders out of consideration for securing postretirement positions. Crisscrossing this three-way, circular power relation are the personal and financial ties based on university affiliations and keiretsu groupings. Actors in this drama cannot be unequivocally categorized. Freely moving in and out of different arenas, they jointly manage the economic affairs of the House of Japan.

The basic pattern of social organization in Japan closely parallels that of a family. Individuals and groups are vertically organized and are emotively related to each other in a complex web of mutual obligations and dependency. The rivalry between hierarchies for status and power provides a basic motivational force. Consensus and compromises among vertically related members of a group, rather than a majority rule among equals, is the basic decision-making principle. The fundamental dichotomies are those involving the inside and the outside, and the basic orientation is that of the above and the below. The public and the private, the central and the local, and the big and the small are all understood essentially as vertical continua.

There is no denying that individual freedom, dignity, and creativity suffer in Japan's hierarchical groupism. There are, however, some merits in groupism that more or less compensate for its shortcomings. Superior productivity of a work group whose members are emotionally tied together and committed to the group's goals is well recognized. Paradoxically, Japanese groupism could be said to be more "egalitarian" than Western individualism, in that a person could find security in a group without possessing economic means or physical attractiveness—which is often a prerequisite to social acceptance in the more individualistic West.

The main focus of this book has been on the central aspects of the

Japanese politicoeconomic system. The peripheries have been merely touched upon. Completely hidden from view, moreover, is the shape and character of the underground world of influence peddlers, gangsters, right-wing terrorists, extortionary journalists, and other shady but powerful characters. The underground and the surface worlds are closely linked with pipelines of profiteering and dirty-money politics. Not much is publicly known in Japan about the workings of the underground world, except that it is widely acknowledged that there is much more than meets the eye.

Another aspect of the Japanese economic system that we did not examine is its international and intercultural dimensions. Parts of the system are organically related to other parts so that, as organs of a human body, they cannot function properly when severed from the whole and connected to another. An acute problem of adjustment arises, for example, when a foreign subsidiary is established in Japan employing a staff of Japanese workers. For the operation of the firm to be successful, the workers must be made to feel that they *belong* to the company, and the company must be linked to the larger community through university, keiretsu, banking, or other ties. A deep understanding of the nature of both the Japanese and non-Japanese ways of doing things is required for a satisfactory solution of such a problem. A more fundamental question, to which the Japanese must address themselves, is this: The Japanese system works reasonably well within its own isolated and closed shells. In the coming years of freer and more open international relations, can the Japanese system, with all its institutional peculiarities, be successfully integrated with other (primarily Western) systems? Institutions that are perfectly in harmony with Japan's own historical, social, and cultural factors may very well be incongruous with the non-Japanese traditions. And the burden of adjustment and accommodation is on the Japanese shoulder, since *they* are a cultural minority in the larger world setting. Although the West may benefit a great deal from learning more about Japan, in the final analysis it is the Japanese themselves who must develop an objective and relative understanding of their own social and economic arrangements and ways.

Index

Index

administrative guidance (*gyosei shido*),
48–49. *See also* guidance cartels;
window guidance
advisory councils, 67–76; ministerial affiliations, 67; nature and characteristics,
67–69; and public pricing, 73–76
age: respect for, 16; and seniority, 35, 107–
108
agency delegation, 57
Agency of Natural Resources and Energy
(MITI), 55
agricultural cooperatives, 156
Allied occupation authorities, 7, 119
amae, 24–25; in corporate organization, 86
amakudari ("descent from heaven"),
44–46, 138
Antimonopoly Law (AML), 131–134; and
FTC, 131; and guidance cartels, 134;
and MITI, 135; and trade associations, 140
ascription, 21, 29–30, 32, 35
authority: and dependency, 24–25; in the
family, 15–16; of state bureaucrats,
39
Azumi, Koya, 34

bakufu (military government), 6
Banking Bureau (MOF), 52, 179
banking system, 150–152
Bank of Japan (BOJ): and Bank Rates,
167–168; and bill-discount market,
159–160; city bank borrowing from,
151; determination of bond interest
rates, 162; as a holder of bonds, 160;
issuance of currency, 52; lending policy, 167–168; market operations,
159–160, 166–167; and Ministry of
Finance, 52, 164–165; 1974 balance
sheet, 167t; organization of, 164;
placements of bills and bonds, 162; as
a quasi-special private bank, 66; regulation of new bond issues, 162; reserve requirement policy, 166; window guidance, 168–169.
Bank of Japan Law, 164
Bank Rates, 167–168
banks, 150–156; and Bill for the Promotion
of Specific Industries, 137; city, 150;
commercial, 152–156; lending to general trading companies, 130; low
equity ratio, 155–156; ordinary, 150;
regional, 150; ten largest, 81t; trust,

151; types of, 150; types of deposits,
154–155
Basic Industries Bureau (MITI), 54
batsu. *See* cliques
Benedict, Ruth, 23
Bieda, K., 144
bill-discount market, 159–160
Bill for the Promotion of Specific Industries,
136–137
blue-collar workers. *See* worker
bond market, 160–163
bonds: local government, 162; general-
account deficit, 162–163; public corporation, 162
bonds and debentures, ownership of, 160–
161
bottom-up decision making, 89–92; and
nenko promotion, 108
budget: general-account, 174–175; international comparison, 172–173; and
Ministry of Finance, 174; special-
account, 174; types of, 174
Budget Bureau (MOF), 50–51, 174, 179
bunke (branch house), 18
bureaucracy, government, 39–58; legislative
power of, 48; ministerial, 42–43;
ministries, 49n
bureaucrats: and *amakudari*, 44–46; elite
(class A), 32, 42–43; former bureaucrats in the Diet, 47–48; as lawmakers,
48; noncareer (class B), 42–43; relations with businessmen and politicians, 39–41, 137; and *shukko*, 46–47,
58; and Tokyo University, 32, 44;
-turned-politicians, 47–48
business-government relations, 40–41,
48–49, 137
business organization: types of, 77; statistics, 79–80
business organizations, 141–142

call loan: dealers, 158–159; market, 158–
159; rates, 159; types of, 158
call money. *See* call loan
career administrators. *See* bureaucrats
cartels: and Antimonopoly Law, 133; types
of, 133–134; in *zaibatsu* organization,
118
Caves, Richard E., 124
central-local government relations. *See*
local government
Central Social Health Insurance Council
(*Chuikyo*), 74–76

185

About the Author

Kanji Haitani is Professor of Economics and Business Administration at State University of New York, Fredonia. Prior to joining the staff of the State University, he had taught for five years at Southern Illinois University at Carbondale. He received the B.A. degree in economics from Ohio Wesleyan University and the Ph.D. degree from the Ohio State University where he majored in economics and minored in sociology. Professor Haitani has contributed articles on international economic relations to journals in several countries, including the *Asian Survey, Kyklos,* and the *Journal of Political Economy.*